ITSM for Windows

A User's Guide to Time Series Modelling and Forecasting

Springer

New York
Berlin
Heidelberg
Barcelona
Budapest
Hong Kong
London
Milan
Paris
Santa Clara
Singapore
Tokyo

Peter J. Brockwell   Richard A. Davis

ITSM for Windows
A User's Guide to Time Series
Modelling and Forecasting

With 63 Illustrations and 2 Diskettes

Written in collaboration with Rob J. Hyndman

 Springer

Peter J. Brockwell
Mathematics Department
Royal Melbourne Institute of Technology
Melbourne, Victoria 3001
Australia

Richard A. Davis
Department of Statistics
Colorado State University
Fort Collins, CO 80523
USA

Library of Congress Cataloging in Publication Data applied for.

Printed on acid-free paper.

Production managed by Ellen Seham; manufacturing supervised by Jacqui Ashri.
Photocomposed copy prepared from the author's LaTeX files.
Printed and bound by Braun-Brumfield, Inc., Ann Arbor, MI.
Printed in the United States of America.

9 8 7 6 5 4 3 2

ISBN 0-387-94337-4 Springer-Verlag New York Berlin Heidelberg
ISBN 3-540-94337-4 Springer-Verlag Berlin Heidelberg New York   SPIN 10555374

Preface

The package **ITSM** (Interactive Time Series Modelling) evolved from the programs for the IBM PC written to accompany our book, *Time Series : Theory and Methods*, published by Springer-Verlag. It owes its existence to the many suggestions for improvements received from users of the earlier programs. Since the release of *ITSM* Version 3.0 in 1991, a large number of further improvements have been made and incorporated into the new versions, *ITSM41* and *ITSM50* , both of which are included with this package. The latter is capable of handling longer series but requires a PC 80386 or later with 8 Mbytes of RAM and an EGA or VGA card. The earlier version *ITSM41* requires only a PC 80286 or later with EGA or VGA. (For precise system requirements, see Section 1.2 on page 2.) The main new features of the programs are summarized below.

- Addition of two new modules, *BURG* and *LONGMEM* for multivariate and long-memory modelling respectively;

- Adaptation of the programs to run either under DOS or under Microsoft Windows (Version 3.1 or later);

- An extremely easy to use menu system in which selections can be made either with arrow-keys, hot-keys or mouse;

- Development of Version 5.0 which permits the analysis of univariate series of length up to 20,000 and multivariate series of length up to 10,000 with as many as 11 components (on computers with 8Mb of RAM);

- Incorporation into the program *PEST* of a number of new features including Hannan-Rissanen estimation of mixed ARMA models, Ljung-Box and McLeod-Li diagnostic statistics, automatic AICC minimization for Yule-Walker and Burg AR models and superposition of the graphs of sample and model spectra and autocovariance functions;

- Incorporation into *SMOOTH* of a frequency-based smoother (which eliminates high-frequency components from the Fourier transform of the data) and automatic selection of the parameter for exponential smoothing;

- Addition of new features (described in Appendix A) to the screen editor *WORD6* .

The package includes the screen editor *WORD6* and eight programs, *PEST*, *SMOOTH*, *SPEC*, *TRANS*, *ARVEC*, *BURG*, *ARAR* and *LONGMEM*, whose functions are summarized in Chapter 1.

If you choose to install the smaller version, *ITSM41*, the corresponding programs *PEST*, *SPEC* and *SMOOTH* can deal with time series of up to 2300 observations and *ARVEC*, *BURG*, *ARAR*, *LONGMEM* and *TRANS* can handle series of lengths 700, 700, 1000, 1000 and 800 respectively. If your PC meets the system requirements, you should load *ITSM50*, which can handle much longer series (20,000 univariate or 10,000 multivariate observations).

We are greatly indebted to many people associated with the development of the programs and manual. Outstanding contributions were made by Joe Mandarino, the architect of the original version of *PEST*, Rob Hyndman, who wrote the original version of the manual for *PEST*, and Anthony Brockwell, who has given us constant support in all things computational, providing *WORD6*, the graphics subroutines, the current menu system and the expertise which made possible the development of Version 5.0. The first version of the *PEST* manual was prepared for use in a short course given by the Key Centre in Statistical Sciences at Royal Melbourne Institute of Technology (RMIT) and The University of Melbourne. We are indebted to the Key Centre for support and for permission to make use of that material. We also wish to thank the National Science Foundation for support of the research on which many of the algorithms are based, R. Schnabel of the University of Colorado computer science department for permission to use his optimization program, and Carolyn Cook for her assistance in the final preparation of an earlier version of the manual. We are grateful for the encouragement provided by Duane Boes and the excellent working environments of Colorado State University, The University of Melbourne and RMIT. The editors of Springer-Verlag have been a constant source of support and encouragement and our families, as always, have played a key role in maintaining our sanity.

Melbourne, Victoria   P.J. Brockwell
Fort Collins, Colorado   R.A. Davis
February, 1994

Contents

1

Introduction

1.1 The Programs

The time series programs described in this manual are all included in the package **ITSM** (Interactive Time Series Modelling) designed to accompany the book *Time Series: Theory and Methods* by Peter Brockwell and Richard Davis, (Springer-Verlag, Second Edition, 1991). With this manual you will find two versions of the package, *ITSM41* and *ITSM50* (each on a $3\frac{1}{2}$" diskette). The system requirements for *ITSM41* are fewer than for *ITSM50* (see Section 1.2), however *ITSM50* can handle larger data sets (univariate series with up to 20000 observations and multivariate series with up to 10000 observations of each of 11 components). Both versions of the package contain the programs listed below.

PEST is a program for the modelling, analysis and forecasting of univariate time series. The name "PEST" is an abbreviation for **P**arameter **EST**imation.

SPEC is a program which performs non-parametric spectral estimation for both univariate and bivariate time series.

SMOOTH permits the user to apply symmetric moving average, exponential or low-pass smoothing operators to a given data set.

TRANS allows the calculation and plotting of sample cross-correlations between two series of equal lengths, and the fitting of a transfer function model to represent the relation between them.

ARVEC uses the Yule-Walker equations to fit vector autoregressive models to multivariate time series with up to 6 components (*ITSM41*) or 11 components (*ITSM50*) and allows automatic order-selection using the AICC criterion.

BURG uses Burg's algorithm to fit autoregressive models to multivariate time series with up to 6 components (*ITSM41*) or 11 components (*ITSM50*) and allows automatic order-selection using the AICC criterion.

ARAR is based on the ARARMA forecasting technique of Newton and Parzen. For a univariate data set it first selects and applies (if necessary) a memory-shortening transformation to the data. It then fits a subset autoregressive model to the memory-shortened series and uses the fitted model to calculate forecasts.

LONGMEM can be used to simulate data from a specified fractionally integrated ARMA model with zero mean. It can also be used to fit such a model to a data set (by maximizing the Whittle approximation to the Gaussian likelihood) and to forecast future values of the series.

This manual is designed to be a practical guide to the use of the programs. For a more extensive discussion of time series modelling and the methods used in **ITSM**, see the book *Time Series: Theory and Methods*, referred to subsequently as *BD*. Information regarding the data sets included with the package is contained in Appendix B. Further details, and in some cases an analysis of the data, can be found in *BD*.

1.2 System Requirements

ITSM41 :

- IBM PC (286 or later) or compatible computer operating under MS-DOS; to run the programs in *WINDOWS*, version 3.1 or later is required;

- at least 540 K of RAM available for applications (to determine your available RAM use the DOS command *mem* and observe *Largest executable program size*); if you have DOS Version 6.0 or later you can optimize your available RAM by running *memmaker*;

- a hard disk with at least 1.1 Mb of space available;

- an EGA or VGA card for graphics;

- a mathematics co-processor (recommended but not essential).

ITSM50 :

- IBM PC (386 or later) or compatible computer operating under MS-DOS; to run the programs in *WINDOWS*, version 3.1 or later is required;

- at least 8 Mb of RAM;

- a hard disk with at least 2.6 Mb of space available;

- an EGA or VGA card for graphics;

- a mathematics co-processor (recommended but not essential).

When booting the computer, the program ANSI.SYS should be loaded. This is done by including the command *DEVICE=ANSI.SYS* in your CONFIG.SYS file.

1.2.1   INSTALLATION

1. Select a version of *ITSM* suitable for your system configuration. To install the programs and data on your hard disk in a directory called `C:\ITSMW`, place the program disk in Drive A and type

   DOS
   Window

   ```
   C:  ←
   A:UNZIP A:ITSMW  ←
   ```

   (other drives may be substituted for `A:` and `C:`). The files on the disk will then be copied into a directory `C:\ITSMW`.

2. We shall assume now that you have installed *ITSM* as in 1 above and are in the directory `C:\ITSMW`.

PRELIMINARIES FOR DOS OPERATION

(If you plan to run the programs under Microsoft Windows go to 4 below.)

3. Before running *ITSM* you will need to load a graphics dump program if you wish to print hard copies of the graphs. This can be done as follows:

   (a) To print graphs on an HP LaserJet printer connected as lpt1:, type

   ```
   HPDUMP 1  ←
   ```

   (b) To print graphs on an HP LaserJet printer connected as lpt2:, type

   ```
   HPDUMP 2  ←
   ```

   (c) To print graphs on an Epson dot matrix printer connected as lpt1: type

   ```
   EPSDUMP  ←
   ```

   (d) To save graphs in a disk file FNAME first execute either a or c above and then type

   ```
   LPTX -o FNAME -1  ←
   ```

   Subsequent output directed to lpt1: is then stored cumulatively in the file FNAME. [To switch off this option, type `LPTX -c` ← .]

   NOTES: If in steps a, b or c you get the message "highres already loaded" it means that one of hpdump 1, hpdump 2 or epsdump has already been loaded and you will need to reboot the computer if you wish to load a different one. If you have an HP LaserJet III printer with 1 Mb or more of optional memory installed, it is essential to set Page Protection on the printer to the appropriate page size or you will get the error message, 21 `PRINT OVERRUN`, and the bottom of the printed graph will be cut off. (See the LaserJet III Printer User's Manual, p. 4.25.)

PRELIMINARIES FOR OPERATION UNDER WINDOWS (3.1 OR LATER)

4. If you wish to run the programs under Microsoft Windows you will first need to carry out the following steps:

  (a) Type

    `C:\ITSMW\INVSCRN` ↩

  This loads the program *invscrn* which will be used for printing graphs and other screen displays. It is convenient to bypass this step by adding the line

    `C:\ITSMW\INVSCRN`

  to your *autoexec.bat* file. This can be done by typing

    `WORD6 C:\AUTOEXEC.BAT` ↩

  and inserting the required line. The modified file must then be saved by holding down the `<Alt>` key while typing `W` and then typing ↩ . To exit from *WORD6* hold down the `<Alt>` key and type `X`. The program *invscrn* will then be automatically loaded each time you boot your computer.

  (If you have installed *ITSM50* , you must also add the line

    `DEVICE=C:\ITSMW\DOSXNT.386`

  immediately below the line

    `[386Enh]`

  of the *system.ini* file in the directory `C:\WINDOWS`. Do this by typing

    `WORD6 C:\WINDOWS\SYSTEM.INI` ↩

  and proceeding as above.)

  (b) Type

    `COPY C:\ITSMW\ITSMWIN.REC C:\WINDOWS` ↩
    `COPY C:\ITSMW\*.ICO C:\WINDOWS` ↩

  (c) Run *WINDOWS* by typing `WIN` ↩

  (d) Double click on the *RECORDER* icon in the *ACCESSORIES* window

  (e) Click on *FILE* in the *RECORDER* window

  (f) Click on the option *OPEN*

  (g) Click on the file name *ITSMWIN.REC*

  (h) Click on *OK*

  (i) Click on *MACRO* in the *RECORDER* window

  (j) Click on *RUN*

You should now see a window labelled *itsmw* containing icons for the *ITSM* modules *PEST*, *SMOOTH*, etc. and the screen editor *WORD6*. To run any one of them, e.g. *WORD6*, double click on the appropriate icon. To exit from the screen editor *WORD6*, hold down the <Alt> key and press X. To terminate the *RECORDER* session, click on the icon labelled *RECORDER-ITSMWIN.REC* and then click on *CLOSE*. In case of difficulty running *ITSMWIN.REC*, the *WINDOWS* installation can be done manually as described below.

You may wish to resize and relocate the *itsmw* window. Once you have done this, you can save the window display as follows. Click on *OPTIONS* in the *PROGRAM MANAGER* window and click on the *SAVE SETTINGS ON EXIT* option so that a check appears beside it. Then exit from *WINDOWS*. When you next run *WINDOWS* by typing WIN you will see the same arrangement of windows, including the *itsmw* window set up previously. To prevent inadvertently changing this arrangement when you next exit from *WINDOWS*, click again on *OPTIONS* in the *PROGRAM MANAGER* window and then click on the *SAVE SETTINGS ON EXIT* option to remove the check mark.

MANUAL SETUP FOR OPERATION UNDER WINDOWS

In case you had trouble running the setup procedure in Step 4 above, here is an alternative but less streamlined procedure to replace it:

(a) Load *invscrn* and (if you are installing *ITSM50*) modify your *system.ini* file as described in 4(a)

(b) Copy the files as in 4(b) and run *WINDOWS* by typing WIN↩

(c) Click on *FILE* in the *PROGRAM MANAGER* window

(d) Click on the option *NEW*

(e) Click on *PROGRAM GROUP*

(f) Click on *OK*

(g) After the heading *DESCRIPTION* type itsmw

(h) Click on *OK* (At this point a window will open with the heading *itsmw*.)

(i) Click again on *FILE* in the *PROGRAM MANAGER* window

(j) Click on *NEW*

(k) Click on *PROGRAM ITEM*

(l) Click on *OK*

(m) After the heading *DESCRIPTION* type pest

(n) After the heading *COMMAND LINE* type C:\ITSMW\PEST.PIF (replace PIF by EXE for *ITSM41*)

(o) After the heading *WORKING DIRECTORY* type `C:\ITSMW`

(p) Click on *CHANGE ICON*

(q) Click on *OK*

(r) Type `PEST.ICO`

(s) Click on *OK*

(t) Click on *OK*

(u) Click on *OK*

The *itsmw* window will now contain an icon labelled *pest*. To run pest, double click on this icon and a title page will appear on the screen. Follow the screen prompts to exit from *PEST* .

Repeat steps (i)–(u), replacing `pest` in (m), (n) and (r) by `smooth`. A second icon will then appear in the *itsmw* window, labelled *smooth*.

Repeat steps (i)–(u) for each of the other modules, *SPEC, TRANS, ARVEC, BURG, ARAR, LONGMEM* and *WORD6*, in each case replacing `pest` in (m), (n) and (r) by the appropriate module name. You should then have nine icons in the *itsmw* window. Each module, e.g. *WORD6*, is run by double clicking on the appropriate icon. To exit from the screen editor *WORD6* hold down the `<Alt>` key and press X.

To save the window display, click on *OPTIONS* in the *PROGRAM MANAGER* window and click on the *SAVE SETTINGS ON EXIT* option so that a check appears beside it. Then exit from *WINDOWS*. When you again run *WINDOWS* by typing `WIN` you will see the same arrangement of windows, including the *itsmw* window set up previously. To prevent inadvertently changing this arrangement when you next exit from *WINDOWS*, click on the *SAVE SETTINGS ON EXIT* option again to remove the check mark.

It is usually advantageous, especially when saving or printing graphs, to run the programs in full-screen mode. Holding down the `<Alt>` key and pressing `<Enter>` toggles the programs between full-screen and window modes.

NOTE. If after installation you select a module and nothing happens, it is very likely that you do not have sufficient RAM available for applications (to check your available RAM, use the DOS command *mem*). To run the *ITSM41* programs under *WINDOWS* you will need a *Largest executable program size* of 537K. To run *ITSM41* under DOS you will need 548K, however the modules can also be run directly from the DOS prompt (by typing PEST↩ , SMOOTH↩ , etc. instead of ITSM↩) in which case 537K of RAM will suffice. If you have DOS 6.0 or later you can optimize your available RAM using the DOS program *memmaker*.

1.2.2 RUNNING ITSM

5. You are now ready to run ITSM. (The preliminary loading of *hpdump* or *epsdump* for DOS operation or of *invscrn* for Windows operation is required only when you boot the computer.)

If you are running the programs in DOS, change the directory to ITSMW by typing

CD \ITSMW↩

Making sure the <Num Lock> key is off, type

ITSM↩

and select a module (e.g. *SMOOTH*) from the *ITSM* menu by highlighting your selection with the arrow keys and pressing ↩ . (If you have an activated mouse, the mouse pointer must be clear of the menu choices before you can use the arrow keys. Depending on your mouse driver, you may be able to use your mouse for menu selection. In case of problems with the mouse, you should deactivate it and use the arrow keys.)

If you are running the programs in *WINDOWS*, double click with the mouse on one of the icons (e.g. *SMOOTH*) located in the *itsmw* window.

When you see the module title enclosed in a box on the screen, press any key to continue, selecting items from the menus as they appear. After exiting from the module *SMOOTH* you can exit from *ITSM* (if you are running in *DOS*) by pressing <F10>.

1.2.3 PRINTING GRAPHS

6. DOS: Assuming you have carried out the appropriate steps described in 3, graphs or text which appear on the screen can be printed (or filed) by pressing <Shift> <Prt Scr> when you see the required screen display. If you chose to file graphics output in *FNAME*, you can print the stored image after exiting from *ITSM* by typing, e.g.,

COPY /B FNAME LPT2:

(assuming you chose 3a and 3d above and now have an HP LaserJet printer connected as lpt2:), or

COPY FNAME LPT2:

(if you chose 3c and 3d above and now have an Epson dot matrix printer connected as lpt2:).

WINDOWS: To print any screen display from *ITSM*, first make sure you are operating in full screen mode (by holding down the <Alt> key and pressing <Enter> if necessary). Then hold down the <Shift> key and press <Print Scrn>. Provided you have loaded the program *invscrn* as described in step 4(a) above, this will cause the screen image to be inverted to black on white. Then press the <Print Scrn> key and the displayed text or graph will be copied to the *CLIPBOARD*. You can transfer it to a document in (for example) Microsoft Write using the commands *EDIT* then *PASTE*. The document containing the graph can be printed on whatever printer you have set up to operate under *WINDOWS* by using the commands *FILE* and *PRINT* in Microsoft Write. To switch between applications in Windows (such as *ITSM* and Microsoft Write), hold down the <Alt> key and press <Tab>.

1.3   Creating Data Files

All data to be used in the programs (except those for *ARVEC* and *BURG*) should be stored in standard ASCII files in column form. That is, each value must be on a separate row. There must also be a blank line at the end of each data file. The programs will read the first item of data from each row. Most of the data sets used in *BD* (and a number of others) are included on the diskettes in this form. Data sets for *ARVEC* and *BURG* are multivariate, with the m components observed at time t stored in row t of the file. (See for example the 150 observations of the bivariate series contained in the file LS2.DAT.)

All data files can be examined and edited using *WORD6* – the screen editor provided on the diskette. New data files can also be created using *WORD6*. For example, to create a data file containing the numbers 1 to 5:

- Double click on the *WORD6* icon (in *WINDOWS*) or type WORD6↩ (in DOS) to invoke the screen editor *WORD6*.

- Then type

$$1↩ 2↩ 3↩ 4↩ 5↩$$

- Hold down the <Alt> key and press W. You will be asked for a filename. Type TEST.DAT↩ . Your new data file consisting of the column of numbers 1 2 3 4 5 will then be stored on your disk under the name TEST.DAT.

- To leave *WORD6*, hold down the <Alt> key again and press X.

- To read your new file, invoke *WORD6* again as above. Then hold down the <Alt> key and press R. You will be asked for a file name. Type TEST.DAT↩ . Your new data file consisting of the column of numbers 1 2 3 4 5 will then be read into *WORD6* and printed on the screen.

For further information on the use of *WORD6* see Appendix A.

2

PEST

2.1 Getting Started

2.1.1 RUNNING PEST

Double click on the icon labelled *pest* in the *itsmw* window (or in DOS type PEST↵ from the C:\ITSMW directory) and you should see the figure displayed in Figure 2.1. Then press any key and you will see the Main Menu of *PEST* as shown in Figure 2.2.

At this stage 7 options are available. Further options will appear in the Main Menu after data are entered.

PEST is menu-driven so that you are required only to make choices between options specified by the program. For example, you can choose the first option of the Main Menu [Data entry; statistics; transformations] by typing the highlighted letter **D**. (In the text, the letter corresponding to the "hot" key for immediate selection of menu options will always be printed in boldface.) This option can also be chosen by moving the highlight bar with the mouse to the first row of the menu and clicking. A third alternative is to move the mouse pointer out of the menu box, use the arrow keys to move the highlight bar and then press ↵ . After selecting this option you will see the Data Menu, from which you can make a further selection, e.g. Load new data set, in the same way. To return to the Main Menu, select the last item of the data menu (e.g. by typing **R**). For the remainder of the book we shall indicate selection of menu items by typing the highlighted letter, but in all cases the other two methods of menu selection can equally well be used.

There are several distinct functions of the program *PEST*. The first is to plot, analyze and possibly transform time series data, the second is to compute properties of time series models, and the third utilizes the previous two in fitting models to data. The latter includes checking that the properties of the fitted model match those of the data in a suitable sense. Having found an appropriate model, we can (for example) then use it in conjunction with the data to forecast future values of the series. Sections 2.2–2.5 and 2.7 of this manual deal with the modelling and analysis of data, while Section 2.6 is concerned with model properties.

It is important to keep in mind the distinction between data and model properties and not to confuse the data with the model. At any particular time *PEST* typically stores one data set and one model (which can be identified using the option [Current model and data file status] of the Main Menu). Rarely (if ever) is a real time series generated by a model as simple

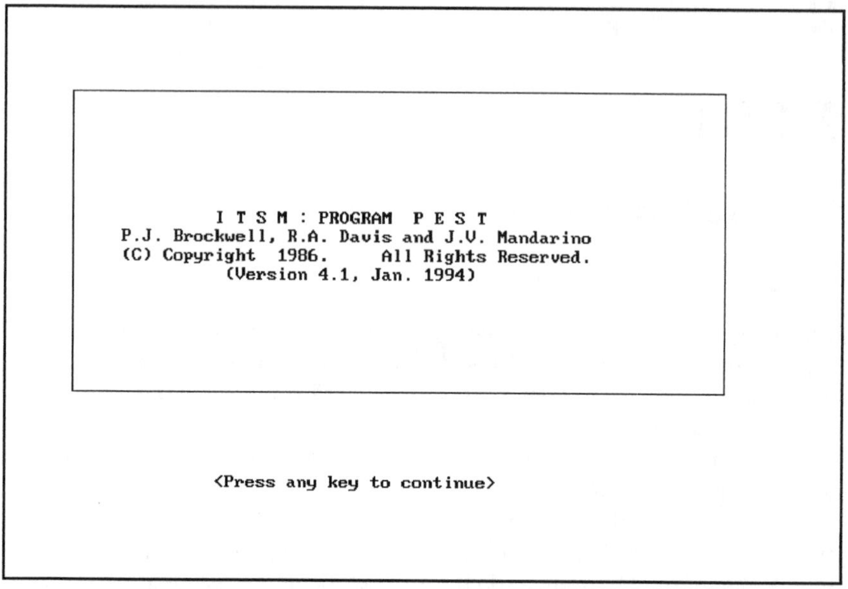

```
              I T S M : PROGRAM  P E S T
     P.J. Brockwell, R.A. Davis and J.V. Mandarino
     (C) Copyright  1986.     All Rights Reserved.
              (Version 4.1, Jan. 1994)




                <Press any key to continue>
```

FIGURE 2.1. *The title page of the program PEST for ITSM41*

as those used for fitting purposes. Our aim is to develop a model which mimics important features of the data, but is still simple enough to be used with relative ease.

2.1.2 PEST TUTORIAL

The examples in this chapter constitute a tutorial session for *PEST* in serialized form. They lead you through a complete analysis of the well-known Airline Passenger Series of Box and Jenkins (see Appendix B).

2.2 Preparing Your Data for Modelling

Once the observed values of your time series are available in a single-column ASCII file (see Section 1.3), you can begin model fitting with *PEST*. The program will read your data from the file, plot it on the screen, compute sample statistics and allow you to do a number of transformations designed to make your transformed data representable as a realization of a zero-mean stationary process.

> EXAMPLE: To illustrate the analysis we shall use the data file AIRPASS.DAT, which contains the number of international airline passengers (in thousands) for each month from Jan '49

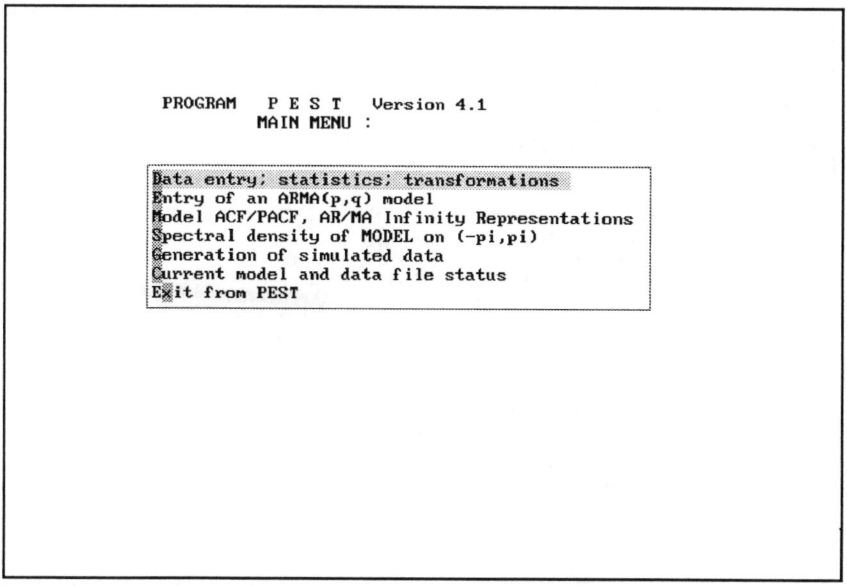

```
PROGRAM   P E S T   Version 4.1
          MAIN MENU :

┌─────────────────────────────────────────────┐
│ Data entry; statistics; transformations      │
│ Entry of an ARMA(p,q) model                   │
│ Model ACF/PACF, AR/MA Infinity Representations│
│ Spectral density of MODEL on (-pi,pi)         │
│ Generation of simulated data                  │
│ Current model and data file status           │
│ Exit from PEST                                │
└─────────────────────────────────────────────┘
```

FIGURE 2.2. *The Main Menu of PEST*

to Dec '60.

2.2.1 ENTERING DATA

From the Main Menu of *PEST* select the first option (**Data entry**; statistics; transformations) by typing **D**. The Data Menu will then appear. Choose Option 1 and you will be asked to confirm that you wish to enter new data. Respond by typing **Y**. A list of data files will then appear (in *ITSM50* you must first use the arrow keys to move the highlight bar to <DATA> and then press ↔ to see the data files). To select a data file for analysis, move the highlight bar to the name of the required file and press ↔ . The program *PEST* will then read in your data and display on the screen the number of observations in the data as well as the first three and last data points.

A new data file can always be imported using Option 1 of the Data Menu. Note however that the previous data file is eliminated from *PEST* each time a new file is read in.

> EXAMPLE: Go through the above steps to read the airline passenger data into *PEST*. The file name is AIRPASS.DAT. Once the file has been read in, the screen should appear as in Figure 2.3.

```
DATA FILE    = AIRPASS.DAT
Number of observations =  144
Sample mean  =     .28030E+03
Sample variance  = .14292E+05
Std.Error(Mean)  = .30881E+02
(square root of (1/n)SUM{(1-!h!/r)acvf(h)}, !h!<r=[sqrt(n)])
```

```
DATA MENU :  ┌─────────────────────────────────────────────┐
             │1. Load new data set                         │
             │2. Plot the data; find mean and variance     │
             │3. Plot sample ACF/PACF of current data file │
             │4. File sample ACF/PACF of current data file │
             │5. Box-Cox transformation  [NOT after 6,7,8] │
             │ ─────────────────────────────────────────── │
             │For Classical Decomposition use 6 and/or 7.  │
             │For Differencing use 8.                      │
             │ ─────────────────────────────────────────── │
             │6. Remove seasonal component   [NOT after 7,8,9] │
             │7. Remove polynomial trend     [NOT after 8 or 9] │
             │8. Difference current data     [NOT after 6,7,or 9] │
             │9. Subtract the mean                         │
             │10. File the current data set                │
             │11. Return to main menu                      │
             └─────────────────────────────────────────────┘
```

FIGURE 2.3. *The **PEST** screen after reading in the file AIRPASS.DAT*

2.2.2 FILING DATA

You may wish to change your data using **PEST** and then store it in another file. At any time before or after transforming the data in **PEST**, the data can be filed by choosing Option 10 from the Data Menu. Do not use the name of a file that already exists or it will be overwritten.

2.2.3 PLOTTING DATA

The first step in the analysis of any time series is to plot the data. With **PEST** the data can be plotted by selecting Option 2 from the Data Menu. This will first produce a histogram of the data; pressing any key then causes a graph of the data vs. time to appear on the screen.

Under the histogram several sample statistics are printed. These are defined as follows:

Mean:

$$\bar{X} = \frac{1}{n} \sum_{i=1}^{n} X_i$$

Standard Deviation:

$$s = \sqrt{\frac{1}{n} \sum_{i=1}^{n} \left(X_i - \bar{X}\right)^2} = \sqrt{\frac{1}{n} \left(\sum_{i=1}^{n} X_i^2 - n\bar{X}^2\right)}$$

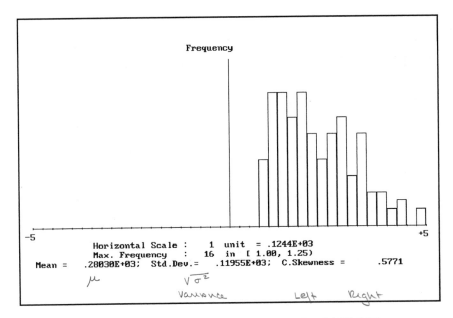

Frequency

-5   +5

Horizontal Scale :   1 unit = .1244E+03
Max. Frequency   :   16 in [1.00, 1.25)
Mean = .28030E+03; Std.Dev.= .11955E+03; C.Skewness =   .5771

μ $\sqrt{\sigma^2}$

Variance   Left   Right

FIGURE 2.4. *The histogram of the series AIRPASS.DAT*

Coefficient of Skewness:

$$\hat{\nu}_3 = \sqrt{\frac{1}{n}\sum_{i=1}^{n}\left(X_i - \bar{X}\right)^3} = \sqrt{\frac{1}{n}\left(\sum_{i=1}^{n}X_i^3 - 3\bar{X}\sum_{i=1}^{n}X_i^2 + 2n\bar{X}^3\right)}$$

EXAMPLE: Continuing with our analysis of the data file AIR-PASS.DAT, choose Option 2 from the Data Menu. The first graph displayed is a histogram of the data, shown in Figure 2.4. Then press any key to obtain the time-plot shown in Figure 2.5. Finally press any key and type **C** to return to the Data Menu.

2.2.4   TRANSFORMING DATA (*BD Sections 1.4, 9.2*)

Transformations are applied in order to produce data which can be successfully modelled as "stationary time series". In particular we need to eliminate trend and cyclic components and to achieve approximate constancy of level and variability with time.

EXAMPLE: The airline passenger data are clearly not stationary. The level and variability both increase with time and there appears to be a large seasonal component (with period 12).

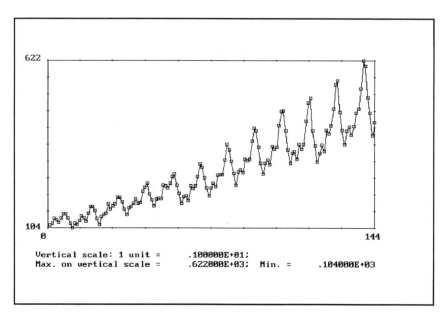

FIGURE 2.5. *The time-plot of the series AIRPASS.DAT*

Non-stationary data must be transformed before attempting to fit a stationary model. *PEST* provides a number of transformations which are useful for this purpose.

BOX-COX TRANSFORMATIONS (*BD Section 9.2*)

Box-Cox transformations can be carried out by selecting Option 5 of the Data Menu. If the original observations are $Y_1, Y_2, \ldots, Y_n$, the Box-Cox transformation f_λ converts them to $f_\lambda(Y_1), f_\lambda(Y_2), \ldots, f_\lambda(Y_n)$, where

$$f(y) = \begin{cases} \frac{y^\lambda - 1}{\lambda}, & \lambda \neq 0, \\ \log(y), & \lambda = 0. \end{cases}$$

These transformations are useful when the variability of the data increases or decreases with the level. By suitable choice of λ, the variability can often be made nearly constant. In particular, for positive data whose standard deviation increases linearly with level, the variability can be stabilized by choosing $\lambda = 0$.

The choice of λ can be made by trial and error, using the graphs of the transformed data which can be plotted using Option 2 of the Data Menu. (After inspecting the graph for a particular λ you can invert the transformation using Option 5 of the Data Menu, after which you can then try another value of λ.) Very often it is found that no transformation is needed or that the choice $\lambda = 0$ is satisfactory.

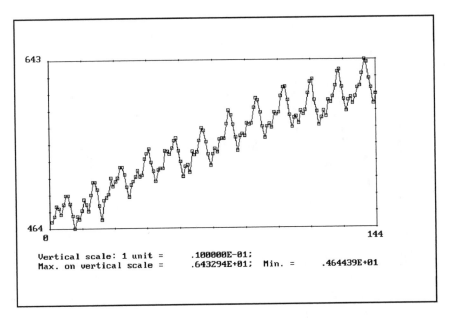

FIGURE 2.6. *The series AIRPASS.DAT after taking logs*

EXAMPLE: For the series AIRPASS.DAT the variability increases with level and the data are strictly positive. Taking natural logarithms (i.e. choosing a Box-Cox transformation with $\lambda = 0$) gives the transformed data shown in Figure 2.6. You can perform this transformation and plot the graph (starting in the Data Menu with the data file AIRPASS.DAT) by typing **5** 0↩ (to transform the data), then **2** ↩ (to plot the graph).

Notice how the variation no longer increases. The seasonal effect remains, as does the upward trend. These will be removed shortly. Since the log transformation has stabilized the variability, it is not necessary to consider other values of λ. Note that the data stored in *PEST* now consists of the natural logarithms of the original data.

CLASSICAL DECOMPOSITION (*BD Section 1.4*)

There are two methods provided in *PEST* for the elimination of trend and seasonality. These are

(i) "classical decomposition" of the series into a trend component, a seasonal component and a random residual component and

(ii) differencing.

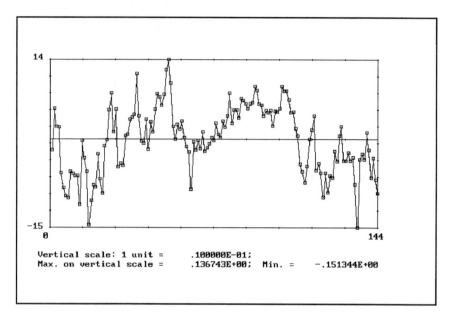

FIGURE 2.7. *The logged AIRPASS.DAT series after classical decomposition*

Classical decomposition of the series $\{X_t\}$ is based on the model,

$$X_t = m_t + s_t + Y_t$$

where X_t is the observation at time t, m_t is a "trend component", s_t is a "seasonal component" and Y_t is a "random noise component" which is stationary with mean zero. The objective is to estimate the components m_t and s_t and subtract them from the data to generate a sequence of residuals (or estimated noise) which can then be modelled as a stationary time series.

To achieve this, select Option 6 then Option 7 from the Data Menu. (You can also estimate trend only or seasonal component only by selecting the appropriate option separately.)

The estimated noise sequence automatically replaces the previous data stored in *PEST*.

> EXAMPLE: The logged airline passenger data has an apparent seasonal component of period 12 (corresponding to the month of the year) and an approximately linear trend. Remove these by typing **6** **12**↩ ↩ **7** **1**↩ (starting from the Data Menu).
>
> Figure 2.7 shows the transformed data (or residuals) Y_t, obtained by classical decomposition of the logged AIRPASS.DAT series. $\{Y_t\}$ shows no obvious deviations from stationarity and it would now be reasonable to attempt to fit a stationary time

series model to this series. We shall not pursue this approach any further in our tutorial, but turn instead to the **differencing** approach. (After completing the tutorial, you should have no difficulty in returning to this point and completing the classical decomposition analysis by fitting a stationary time series model to $\{Y_t\}$.)

Restore the original airline passenger data into *PEST* by using Option 1 of the Data Menu and reading in the file AIRPASS.DAT.

DIFFERENCING (*BD Sections 1.4, 9.1, 9.6*)

Differencing is a technique which can also be used to remove seasonal components and trends. The idea is simply to consider the differences between pairs of observations with appropriate time-separations. For example, to remove a seasonal component of period 12 from the series $\{X_t\}$, we generate the transformed series,

$$Y_t = X_t - X_{t-12}.$$

It is clear that all seasonal components of period 12 are eliminated by this transformation, which is called **differencing at lag 12**. A linear trend can be eliminated by differencing at lag 1, and a quadratic trend by differencing twice at lag 1 (i.e. differencing once to get a new series, then differencing the new series to get a second new series). Higher-order polynomials can be eliminated analogously. It is worth noting that differencing at lag 12 not only eliminates seasonal components with period 12 but also any linear trend.

Repeated differencing can be done with *PEST* by selecting Option 8 from the Data Menu.

> EXAMPLE: At this stage of the analysis we have restored the original data set AIRPASS.DAT into *PEST* with the Data Menu displayed on the screen. Type **5 0**↩ to replace the stored observations by their natural logs. The transformed series can now be deseasonalized by differencing at lag 12. To do this type **8 12**↩ . Inspection of the graph of the deseasonalized series suggests a further differencing at lag 1 to eliminate the remaining trend. To do this type **8 1**↩ . Then type **2** ↩ and you should see the transformed and twice differenced series shown in Figure 2.8.

SUBTRACTING THE MEAN

The term *ARMA* model is used in this manual (and in *BD*) to mean a stationary zero mean process satisfying the defining difference equations

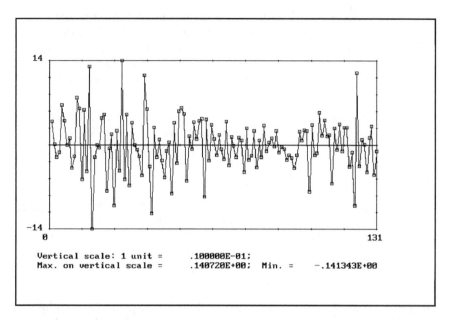

FIGURE 2.8. *The series AIRPASS.DAT after taking logs and differencing at lags 12 and 1*

in Section 2.6.1. In order to fit such a model to data, the sample-mean of the data should therefore be small. (An estimate of the standard error of the sample mean is displayed on the screen just after reading in the data file (see Figure 2.3).) Once the apparent deviations from stationarity of the data have been removed, we therefore (in most cases) subtract the sample mean of the transformed data from each observation to generate a series to which we then fit a zero-mean stationary model. Effectively we are estimating the mean of the model by the sample mean, then fitting a (zero-mean) ARMA model to the "mean-corrected" transformed data. If we know a priori that the observations are from a process with zero mean then this process of mean correction is omitted. *PEST* keeps track of all the transformations (including mean correction) which are made. You can check these for yourself by going to Option 10 of the Main Menu. When it comes time to predict the original series, *PEST* will invert all these transformations automatically.

> EXAMPLE: Subtract the mean of the transformed and twice differenced AIRPASS.DAT series by typing **9**. Type **R** to return to the Main Menu, then **C** to check the status of the data and model which currently reside in *PEST*. You will see in particular that the default white noise model (ARMA(0,0)) with variance 1 is displayed since no model has yet been entered.

2.3   Finding a Model for Your Data

After transforming the data (if necessary) as described in Section 2.2.4, we are now in a position to fit a zero-mean stationary time series model. *PEST* restricts attention to ARMA models (see Section 2.6.1). These constitute a very large class of zero-mean stationary time series. By appropriate choice of the parameters of an ARMA process $\{X_t\}$, we can arrange for the covariances $\text{Cov}(X_{t+h}, X_t)$ to be arbitrarily close, for all h, to the corresponding covariances $\gamma(h)$ of any stationary series with $\gamma(0) > 0$ and $\lim_{h\to\infty} \gamma(h) = 0$. But how do we find the most appropriate ARMA model for a given series? *PEST* uses a variety of tools to guide us in the search. These include the ACF (autocorrelation function), the PACF (partial autocorrelation function) and the AICC statistic (a bias-corrected form of Akaike's AIC statistic, see *BD Section 9.3*).

2.3.1   THE ACF AND PACF (*BD Sections 1.3, 3.3, 3.4, 8.2*)

The **autocorrelation function (ACF)** of the stationary time series $\{X_t\}$ is defined as

$$\rho(h) = \text{Corr}(X_{t+h}, X_t) \quad \text{for } h = 0, \pm 1, \pm 2, \ldots$$

(Clearly $\rho(h) = \rho(-h)$ if X_t is real-valued, as we assume throughout.)

The ACF is a measure of dependence between observations as a function of their separation along the time axis. *PEST* estimates this function by computing the **sample autocorrelation function**, $\hat{\rho}(h)$ of the data $x_1, \ldots, x_n$, i.e.

$$\hat{\rho}(h) = \hat{\gamma}(h)/\hat{\gamma}(0), \ 0 \le h < n,$$

where $\hat{\gamma}(\cdot)$ is the **sample autocovariance function**,

$$\hat{\gamma}(h) = n^{-1} \sum_{j=1}^{n-h} (x_{j+h} - \overline{x})(x_j - \overline{x}), \ 0 \le h < n.$$

Option 3 of the Data Menu can be used to compute and plot the sample ACF for values of the lag h from 1 up to 40. Values which decay rapidly as h increases indicate short term dependency in the time series, while slowly decaying values indicate long term dependency. For ARMA fitting it is desirable to have a sample ACF which decays fairly rapidly (see *BD Chapter 9*). A sample ACF which is positive and very slowly decaying suggests that the data may have a trend. A sample ACF with very slowly damped periodicity suggests the presence of a periodic seasonal component. In either of these two cases you may need to transform your data before continuing (see Section 2.2.4).

Another useful diagnostic tool is the **sample partial autocorrelation function** or sample PACF.

The partial autocorrelation function (PACF) of the stationary time series $\{X_t\}$ is defined (at lag $h > 0$) as the correlation between the residuals of X_{t+h} and X_t after linear regression on $X_{t+1}, X_{t+2}, \ldots, X_{t+h-1}$. This is a measure of the dependence between X_{t+h} and X_t after removing the effect of the intervening variables $X_{t+1}, X_{t+2}, \ldots, X_{t+h-1}$. The sample PACF is estimated from the data $x_1, \ldots, x_n$ as described in *BD Section 3.4*.

The sample ACF and PACF are computed and plotted by choosing Option 3 of the Data Menu. *PEST* will prompt you to specify the maximum lag required. This is restricted by *PEST* to be less than or equal to 40. (As a rule of thumb, the estimates are reliable for lags up to about $\frac{1}{3}$ of the sample size. It is clear from the definition of the sample ACF, $\hat{\rho}(h)$, that it will be a very poor estimator of $\rho(h)$ for h close to the sample size n.)

Once you have specified the maximum lag, M, the sample ACF and PACF values will be plotted on the screen for lags h from 0 to M. The horizontal lines on the graph display the bounds $\pm 1.96/\sqrt{n}$ which are approximate 95% bounds for the autocorrelations of a white noise sequence. If the data is a (large) sample from an independent white noise sequence, approximately 95% of the sample autocorrelations should lie between these bounds. Large or frequent excursions from the bounds suggest that we need a model to explain the dependence and sometimes suggest the kind of model we need (see below). Press any key and the numerical values of the sample ACF and PACF will be printed below the graphs. Press any key again to return to the Data Menu.

The ACF and PACF may be filed for later use using Option 4.

The graphs of the sample ACF and PACF sometimes suggest an appropriate ARMA model for the data.

Suppose that the data $x_1, \ldots, x_n$ are in fact observations of the MA(q) process,

$$X_t = Z_t + \theta_1 Z_{t-1} + \cdots + \theta_q Z_{t-q}$$

where $\{Z_t\}$ is a sequence of uncorrelated random variables with mean 0 and variance σ^2. The ACF of $\{X_t\}$ vanishes for lags greater than q and so the plotted sample ACF of the data should be negligible (apart from sampling fluctuations) for lags greater than q. As a rough guide, if the sample ACF falls between the plotted bounds $\pm 1.96/\sqrt{n}$ for lags $h > q$ then an MA(q) model is suggested.

Analogously, suppose that the data are observations of the AR(p) process defined by

$$X_t = \phi_1 X_{t-1} + \cdots + \phi_p X_{t-p} + Z_t.$$

The PACF of $\{X_t\}$ vanishes for lags greater than p and so the plotted sample PACF of the data should be negligible (apart from sampling fluctuations) for lags greater than p. As a rough guide, if the sample PACF falls between the plotted bounds $\pm 1.96/\sqrt{n}$ for lags $h > p$ then an AR(p) model is suggested.

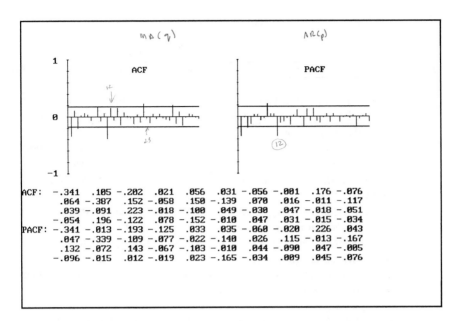

FIGURE 2.9. *Sample ACF and PACF of the transformed AIRPASS.DAT series*

If neither the sample ACF nor PACF "cuts off" as in the previous two paragraphs, a more refined model selection technique is required (see the discussion of the AICC statistic in Section 2.3.4 below). Even if the sample ACF or PACF does cut off at some lag, it is still advisable to explore models other than those suggested by the sample ACF and PACF values.

> EXAMPLE: Figure 2.9 shows the ACF and PACF for the AIR-PASS.DAT series after taking logarithms, differencing at lags 12 and 1 and subtracting the mean. These graphs suggest we consider an MA model of order 12 (or perhaps 23) with a large number of zero coefficients, or alternatively an AR model of order 12.

2.3.2 ENTERING A MODEL

To do any serious analysis with *PEST*, a model must be entered. This can be done either by specifying an ARMA model directly using the option [Entry of an ARMA(p,q) model] or (if the program contains a data file which is to be modelled as an ARMA process) by using the option [Preliminary estimation of ARMA parameters] of the Main Menu. If no model is entered, *PEST* assumes the default ARMA(0,0) or white noise model,

$$X_t = Z_t,$$

where $\{Z_t\}$ is an uncorrelated sequence of random variables with mean zero and variance one.

If you have data and no particular ARMA model in mind, it is best to let *PEST* find the model by using the option [Preliminary estimation of ARMA parameters].

Sometimes you may wish to try a model used in a previous session with *PEST* or a model suggested by someone else. In that case use the option [Entry of an ARMA(p,q) model].

A particularly useful feature of the latter option is the ability to import a model stored in an earlier session. *PEST* can read the stored model, saving you the trouble of repeating an optimization or entering the model coefficient by coefficient.

To enter a model directly, specify the order of the autoregressive and moving average polynomials as requested. You will then be required to enter the coefficients. Initially *PEST* will set the white noise variance to 1. To enter a model stored in a file, choose the autoregressive order to be -1.

After you have entered the model, you will see the Model Menu which gives you the opportunity to make any required changes.

If you wish to alter a specific coefficient in the model, enter the number of the coefficient. The autoregressive coefficients are numbered 1, 2, ..., p and the moving average coefficients are numbered $p+1, p+2, \ldots, p+q$. For example, to change the 2nd moving average coefficient in an ARMA(3,2) model, type **C** to change a coefficient and then type **5**↩ .

2.3.3 PRELIMINARY PARAMETER ESTIMATION (*BD Sections 8.1–8.5*)

The option [Preliminary estimation of ARMA parameters] of the Main Menu contains fast (but somewhat rough) model-fitting algorithms. These are useful for suggesting the most promising models for the data, but they should be followed by the more refined maximum likelihood estimation procedure in the option [ARMA parameter estimation] of the Main Menu. The fitted preliminary model is generally used as an initial approximation with which to start the non-linear optimization carried out in the course of maximizing the (Gaussian) likelihood.

The AR and MA orders p and q of the model to be fitted must be entered first (see Section 2.6.1). For pure AR models, the preliminary estimation option of *PEST* offers you a choice between the Burg and Yule-Walker estimates. The Burg estimates frequently give higher values of the Gaussian likelihood than the Yule-Walker estimates. For the case $q > 0$, *PEST* will also give you a choice between the two preliminary estimation methods based on the Hannan-Rissanen procedure and the innovations algorithm. If you choose the innovations option by typing **I**, a default value of m will be displayed on the screen. This is a parameter required in the estimation algorithm (discussed in *BD Sections 8.3–8.4*). The standard choice is the default value of m computed by *PEST*.

Once the values of p, q and m have been entered, *PEST* will quickly estimate the parameters of the specified model and display a number of useful diagnostic statistics.

The estimated parameters are given with the ratio of each estimate to 1.96 times its standard error. The denominator (1.96 × standard error) is the critical value for the coefficient. Thus if the ratio is greater than one in absolute value, we may conclude (at level 0.05) that the corresponding coefficient is different from zero. On the other hand, a ratio less than one in absolute value suggests the possibility that the corresponding coefficient in the model may be zero. (If the innovations option is chosen, the ratios of estimates to 1.96 × standard error are displayed only when $p = q$.)

After the estimated coefficients are displayed on the screen, press any key and *PEST* will then do one of two things depending on whether or not the fitted model is causal (see Section 2.6.1).

If the model is causal, *PEST* will give an estimate $\hat{\sigma}^2$ of the white noise variance, $\mathrm{Var}(Z_t)$, and some further diagnostic statistics. These are $-2 \ln L(\hat{\boldsymbol{\phi}}, \hat{\boldsymbol{\theta}}, \hat{\sigma}^2)$, where L denotes the Gaussian likelihood (see *BD equation (8.7.4)*), and the AICC statistic,

$$-2 \ln L + 2(p + q + 1)n/(n - p - q - 2),$$

(see Section 2.3.4 below).

Our eventual aim is to find a model with as small an AICC value as possible. Smallness of the AICC value computed in the option [**Preliminary estimation**] is indicative of a good model, but should be used only as a rough guide. Final decisions between models should be based on maximum likelihood estimation computed in the option [**ARMA parameter estimation**], since for fixed p and q, the values of $\boldsymbol{\phi}, \boldsymbol{\theta}$ and σ^2 which minimize the AICC statistic are the maximum likelihood estimates, not the preliminary estimates. In the option [**Preliminary estimation**] of the Main Menu, it is possible to minimize the AICC for pure autoregressive models fitted either by Burg's algorithm or the Yule-Walker equations by entering -1 as the selected autoregressive order. Autoregressions of all orders up to 26 will then be fitted by the chosen algorithm and the model with smallest AICC value will be selected.

If the preliminary fitted model is non-causal, *PEST* will set all coefficients to .001 to generate a causal model with the specified values of p and q. Further investigation of this model must then be done with the option [**ARMA parameter estimation**].

After completing the preliminary estimation, *PEST* will store the fitted model coefficients and white noise variance. The stored estimate of the white noise variance is the sum of squares of the residuals (or one-step prediction errors) divided by the number of observations.

At this point you can try a different model, file the current model or return to the Main Menu. When you return to the Main Menu, the most recently fitted preliminary model will be stored in *PEST*. You will now see a large number of options available on the Main Menu.

> EXAMPLE: Let us first find the minimum-AICC AR model for the logged, differenced and mean-corrected AIRPASS.DAT series currently stored in *PEST*. From the Main Menu type **P** and then type -1↩ for the order of the autoregression. Type **Y** to select the Yule-Walker estimation procedure. The minimum-AICC AR model is of order 12 with an AICC value of -458.13. Now let us fit a preliminary MA(25) model to the same data set. Select the option [**Try another model**] and type 0↩ for the order of the autoregressive polynomial and 25↩ for the order of the moving average polynomial. Choose the Innovations estimation procedure by typing **I** and type **N** to use the default value for m, the number of autocovariances used in the estimation procedure.
>
> The ratios, (estimated coefficient)/(1.96×standard error), indicate that the coefficients at lags 1 and 12 are non-zero, as we suspected from the ACF. The estimated coefficients at lags 3 and 23 also look substantial even though the corresponding ratios are less than 1 in absolute value.
>
> The displayed values are shown in Figure 2.10. Press any key to see the value of the white noise variance.
>
> Press ↩ once again to display the values of $-2\ln L$ and the AICC. After pressing ↩ , you can return to the Main Menu by typing **R** with the fitted MA(25) model now stored in *PEST*. Note that at this stage of the modelling process the fitted AR(12) model has a smaller AICC value than the MA(25) model. Later we shall find a subset MA(25) model which has an even smaller AICC value.

2.3.4 THE AICC STATISTIC (*BD Sections 9.2, 9.3*)

One measure of the "goodness of fit" of a model is the Gaussian likelihood of the observations under the fitted model. (i.e. the joint probability density, evaluated at the observed values, of the random variables $X_1, \ldots, X_n$, assuming that the fitted model is correct and the white noise is Gaussian.) At first glance, maximization of the Gaussian likelihood seems a plausible criterion for deciding between rival candidates for "best" model to represent a given data set. For fixed p and q, maximization of the (Gaussian) likelihood is indeed a good criterion and is the primary method used for estimation in the option [**ARMA parameter estimation**] of the Main Menu.

The problem with using the likelihood to choose between models of different orders is that for any given model, we can always find one with

```
MA COEFFICIENTS
    -.3567584        .0673203       -.1628928       -.0414917        .1267971
     .0264303        .0282778       -.0647944        .1326293       -.0761577
    -.0066283       -.4987471        .1780694       -.0317712        .1475751
    -.1460599        .0439758       -.0225709       -.0748716       -.0455962
    -.0204091       -.0085370        .2013822       -.0767226       -.0789431
RATIO OF COEFFICIENTS TO (1.96*STANDARD ERROR)
    -2.0833100       .3702629       -.8941181       -.2251240        .6874609
     .1423154        .1522181       -.3486669        .7124265       -.4060748
    -.0352571      -2.6528780        .8623497       -.1522101        .7067652
    -.6944412        .2076199       -.1064952       -.3332041       -.2147060
    -.0960385       -.0401669        .9474893       -.3563148       -.3659467
<Press any key to continue>
```

FIGURE 2.10. *Coefficients of the preliminary MA(25) model*

equal or greater likelihood by increasing either p or q. For example, given the maximum likelihood AR(10) model for a given data set, we can find an AR(20) model for which the likelihood is at least as great. Any improvement in the likelihood however is offset by the additional estimation errors introduced. The AICC statistic allows for this by introducing a penalty for increasing the number of model parameters. The AICC statistic for the model with parameters p, q, ϕ, θ, and σ^2 is defined as

$$AICC(\phi, \theta, \sigma^2) = -2\ln L(\phi, \theta, \sigma^2) + 2(p + q + 1)n/(n - p - q - 2),$$

and a model chosen according to the AICC criterion minimizes this statistic. (The AICC value is a bias-corrected modification of the AIC statistic, $-2\ln L + 2(p + q)$, see *BD Section 9.3*.)

Model selection statistics other than AICC are also available. A Bayesian modification of the AIC statistic, known as the BIC statistic is also computed in the option [**ARMA parameter estimation**]. It is used in the same way as the AICC.

An exhaustive search for a model with minimum AICC or BIC value can be very slow. For this reason the sample ACF and PACF and the preliminary estimation techniques described above are useful in narrowing down the range of models to be considered more carefully in the maximum-likelihood estimation stage of model fitting.

```
The datafile is AIRPASS.DAT              ;  Total data points=   131

Box-Cox transformation applied with lambda =   .00

Difference      lag
    1           12
    2            1

The subtracted mean is            .0003

THE ARMA( 0,25) MODEL IS   X(t) = Z(t)
+(  -.357)*Z(t- 1)  +(    .067)*Z(t- 2)  +(  -.163)*Z(t- 3)  +(  -.041)*Z(t- 4)
+(   .127)*Z(t- 5)  +(    .026)*Z(t- 6)  +(   .028)*Z(t- 7)  +(  -.065)*Z(t- 8)
+(   .133)*Z(t- 9)  +(  -.076)*Z(t-10)  +(  -.007)*Z(t-11)  +(  -.499)*Z(t-12)
+(   .178)*Z(t-13)  +(  -.032)*Z(t-14)  +(   .148)*Z(t-15)  +(  -.146)*Z(t-16)
+(   .044)*Z(t-17)  +(  -.023)*Z(t-18)  +(  -.075)*Z(t-19)  +(  -.046)*Z(t-20)
+(  -.020)*Z(t-21)  +(  -.009)*Z(t-22)  +(   .201)*Z(t-23)  +(  -.077)*Z(t-24)
+(  -.079)*Z(t-25)
         *MODEL NOT INVERTIBLE*

White noise variance =     .115169E-02
AICC               =  -.440927E+03
   <Press any key to continue>
```

FIGURE 2.11. *The PEST screen after choosing the option* [Current model and data file status]

2.3.5 CHANGING YOUR MODEL

The model currently stored by the program and the status of the data file can be checked at any time using the option [Current model and data file status] of the Main Menu. Any parameter can be changed with this option, including the white noise variance, and the model can be filed for use at some other time.

> EXAMPLE: We shall now set some of the coefficients in the current model to zero. To do this choose the option [Current model and data file status] from the the Main Menu by typing C. The resulting screen display is shown in Figure 2.11.
>
> The preliminary estimation in Section 2.3.3 suggested that the most significant coefficients in the fitted MA(25) model were those at lags 1, 3, 12 and 23. Let us therefore try setting all the other coefficients to zero. To change the lag-2 coefficient, select [Change a coefficient] from the menu and enter its number followed by the new value, 0, i.e. press return and type C 2↩ 0↩ . Repeat for each coefficient to be changed. The screen should then look like Figure 2.12. Type R to return to the Main Menu.

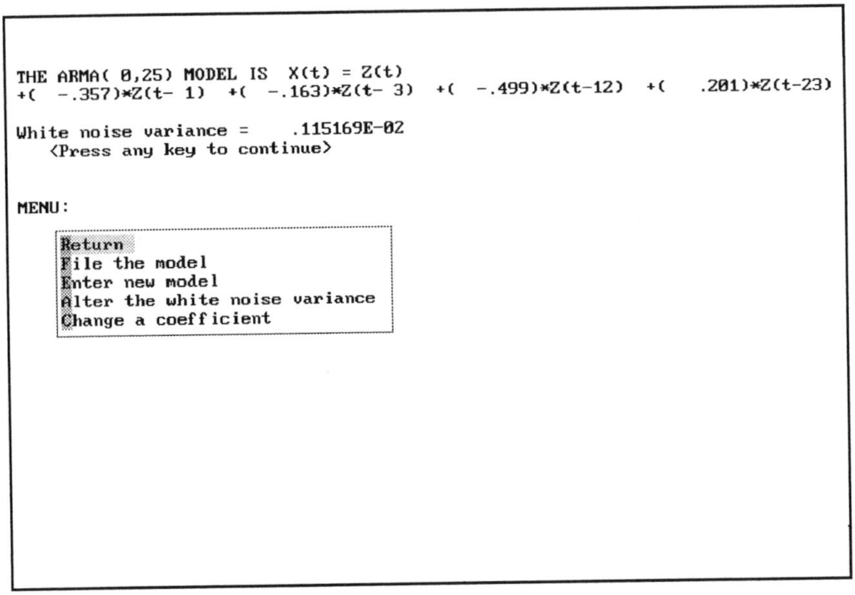

```
THE ARMA( 0,25) MODEL IS   X(t) = Z(t)
+(  -.357)*Z(t- 1)  +(  -.163)*Z(t- 3)  +(  -.499)*Z(t-12)  +(   .201)*Z(t-23)

White noise variance =    .115169E-02
   <Press any key to continue>


MENU:

   Return
   File the model
   Enter new model
   Alter the white noise variance
   Change a coefficient
```

FIGURE 2.12. *The PEST screen after setting coefficients to zero*

2.3.6   PARAMETER ESTIMATION; THE GAUSSIAN LIKELIHOOD (*BD Section 8.7*)

Once you have specified values of p and q and possibly set some coefficients to zero, you can use the full power of *PEST* to estimate parameters. For efficient parameter estimation you must use the option [ARMA parameter estimation] of the Main Menu.

From the Main Menu type **A** to obtain the Estimation Menu displayed in Figure 2.13.

Much of the information displayed in this menu concerns the optimization settings. For most purposes you will need to use the default settings only. (With the default settings, any coefficients which are set to zero will be treated as fixed values and not as parameters. If you wish to include a particular coefficient in the parameters to be optimized you must therefore not set its initial value equal to zero.)

To find the maximum likelihood estimates of your parameters choose the option [Optimize with current settings] by typing **O**. *PEST* will then try to find the parameters which maximize the likelihood of your model with respect to all the non-zero coefficients in the model currently stored by *PEST*.

If you wish to compute the Gaussian likelihood (or one-step predictors and residuals) without doing any optimization, type **L** to select the option [Likelihood of Model (no optimization)].

```
ESTIMATION MENU:

        Help
        Likelihood of Model (no optimization)
        Optimize with current settings
        New Accuracy Parameter
        Set the Maximum No. of Iterations
        Constrain Optimized Coefficients (e.g. for Multiplicative Model)
        Alter Convergence Criterion for th(n,j)
        Method of Estimation
        Return to Main Menu
```

FIGURE 2.13. *The Estimation Menu*

EXAMPLE: Let us find the maximum likelihood estimates of the parameters in the current model for the logged, differenced and mean-corrected airline passenger data stored in *PEST* . Starting from the Main Menu type **A** ↩ and you will see the Estimation Menu. Choose the default option by typing **O**. After a short delay the iterations will cease and you will see the the message

STOPPING VALUE 2 : WITHIN ACCURACY LEVEL

The stopping value of 2 indicates that the minimum of $-2\ln L$ has been located with the specified accuracy. The fitted model is displayed in Figure 2.14. If you see the message

STOPPING VALUE 4 : ITERATION LIMIT EXCEEDED

then the minimum of $-2\ln L$ could not be located with the number of iterations (50) allowed. You can continue the search (starting from the point at which the iterations were inter- rupted) by typing **C** to return to the Estimation Menu, then typing **O** as before.

CHANGING THE OPTIMIZATION SETTINGS

There are several options in the Estimation Menu which enable you to alter the way in which the optimization is carried out. In particular, it is possible to input a new accuracy parameter a (Option **N**), set the maximum number

```
THE ARMA( 0,25) MODEL IS  X(t) = Z(t)
+(  -.355)*Z(t- 1)  +(  -.201)*Z(t- 3)  +(  -.523)*Z(t-12)  +(   .242)*Z(t-23)

   MOVING AVERAGE PARAMETERS :
    THETA( 1)=      -.35528650       THETA( 3)=     -.20131570
    THETA(12)=      -.52297480       THETA(23)=      .24152310

   WHITE NOISE VARIANCE =           .125024E-02
   <Press any key to continue>
   BIC STATISTIC      =          -487.613800
   -2 ln(LIKELIHOOD)  =          -496.517400
   AICC STATISTIC     =          -486.037400  LAST=          -440.926900

    # FUNCTION CALLS =      46 :# ITERATIONS =   5;ACCURACY PARAM.=  .002053
    STOPPING VALUE  2 : WITHIN ACCURACY LEVEL
   <Press any key to continue>
```

FIGURE 2.14. *The maximum likelihood estimates for the transformed AIR-PASS.DAT series*

of iterations m (Option **S**), alter the convergence criterion c (Option **A**) and change the method of optimization (Option **M**). By far the most frequently used option is **O**, however it is a good idea to conclude the estimation with a further optimization using a smaller accuracy parameter.

The following options on the Estimation Menu can be used to alter the optimization settings.

Help

This option prints several hints for using the optimizer.

New Accuracy Parameter

Allows you to enter a new accuracy parameter a between 0 and 1. Reducing a gives more accurate optimization.

Set the Maximum No. of Iterations

Changes the maximum number of iterations m required before terminating the search. Reducing m terminates the search after fewer iterations.

Constrain Optimized Coefficients (e.g. for Multiplicative Model)

Unless you specify otherwise, *PEST* will optimize only the non-zero coefficients in the current model. Sometimes you may not want this. This option enables you to specify constraints on the coefficients to be optimized. Coefficients can be set to non-zero constant values and coefficients which are currently zero can be treated as parameters and included in the optimization. It is also possible to specify optimization subject to multiplicative relationships between the parameters (see below under Multiplicative Models).

Alter Convergence Criterion for th(n,j)

Changes the convergence criterion c. Setting $c = 0$ gives the exact likelihood but setting c to be small (say 0.0005) will usually give an almost identical value with far less computation.

Method of Estimation

Toggles the method of optimization between Maximum Likelihood (the default option) and Least Squares.

STOPPING NUMBER

Each time the optimizing iterations cease, the resulting model will be displayed on the screen with a "stopping number" indicating the conditions under which the search was terminated. The stopping numbers have the following meanings:

1. The relative gradient of the surface is close to zero.

2. Successive iterations did not change any of the optimized parameters by more than the required accuracy parameter a.

3. The last step failed to locate a better point. Either the value is an approximate local minimum or the model is too non-linear at this point – perhaps because of a root near the unit circle. Try different initial values.

4. The iteration limit (m) was reached. (Continue optimization by entering **S** from the results screen then entering **L** again.)

5. The step-size of the search has grown too large. Try different initial values.

    EXAMPLE: In the optimization just completed, stopping number 2 appeared after 5 iterations.

MULTIPLICATIVE MODELS (*BD Section 9.6*)

The option [Constrain Optimized Coefficients] of the Estimation Menu allows the imposition of more complicated constraints on the parameters. Multiplicative models are handled by specifying multiplicative relationships between the ARMA coefficients. For example the multiplicative ARMA model,

$$(1 - aB)X_t = (1 + cB)(1 + dB^{12})Z_t,$$

is fitted as follows. After entering the data (and transforming if necessary), use the option [Entry of an ARMA(p,q) model] of the Main Menu to enter the ARMA(1,13) model with all coefficients zero except the AR coefficient and the MA coefficients at lags 1, 12 and 13. These may be set initially to .001 (or some better non-zero initial values obtained for example from the preliminary estimation option of *PEST*). We then choose the option [ARMA parameter estimation] and enter the following sequence of letters and numbers:

C (To constrain the optimized coefficients),

D (To define multiplicative relationships),

1↩ (The number of multiplicative relationships),

2↩ 13↩ 14↩ (To indicate that the 14th coefficient is constrained to be the product of the 2nd and 13th),

R (To return to the Optimization Menu), and finally

O (To optimize with the current settings).

HINTS FOR ADVANCED USERS

- You can optimize with respect to as many as 52 coefficients.

- If the optimization search takes the MA coefficients outside the invertible region you can convert the model to an equivalent (from a second-order point of view) invertible model. See Section 2.3.7 for further information about switching to invertible models. *PEST* (unlike some programs) has no difficulty in computing Gaussian likelihoods and best linear predictors for non-invertible models.

- For complicated or high-order models be sure to try a variety of initial values to check that you are not finding a local rather than a global minimum of $-2\ln L$.

- You cannot keep constant the 3rd coefficient in a multiplicative relationship (i.e. the product of the first 2).

2.3.7   OPTIMIZATION RESULTS

After running the optimization algorithm, *PEST* displays the model parameters (coefficients and white noise variance), the values of $-2\ln L$, AICC, and BIC, information regarding the computations, and the Results Menu.

EXAMPLE: Figure 2.14 shows the *PEST* screen after completing optimization for the logged, differenced and mean-corrected series AIRPASS.DAT, using an MA(23) model with non-zero coefficients at lags 1, 3, 12 and 23.

The next stage of the analysis is to consider a variety of competing models and to select the most suitable. The following table shows the AICC statistics for a variety of subset moving average models of order less than 24.

	Lags				AICC
1	3		12		23	-486.04
1	3		12	13	23	-485.78
1	3	5	12		23	-489.95 ✓
1	3		12	13		-482.62
1			12			-475.91

The best of these models from the point of view of AICC value is the one with non-zero coefficients at lags 1, 3, 5, 12 and 23. To substitute this model for the one currently stored in *PEST* (starting from the Results Menu), type

$$\mathbf{C} \hookleftarrow \mathbf{C}\ \mathbf{C}\ 1 \hookleftarrow 5 \hookleftarrow \mathbf{R} \hookleftarrow \mathbf{O}$$

and optimization will begin as before. You should obtain the non-invertible model (*BD Example 9.2.2*),

$$X_t = Z_t - .439Z_{t-1} - .302Z_{t-3} + .242Z_{t-5}$$
$$-.656Z_{t-12} + .348Z_{t-23}, \quad \{Z_t\} \sim \text{WN}(0, .00103)$$

For future reference, store the model under the filename AIR-PASS.MOD using the option [Store the Model] of the Results Menu.

We have seen in our example how, when optimizing iterations cease, the stopping code indicates whether or not more iterations are required. The display of results which includes this information also contains a menu which allows us to investigate properties of the fitted model, including its goodness of fit. The options available in the Results Menu are described below.

Store the Model
It is wise to file the fitted model, particularly if it was the result of a time-consuming optimization as in the previous example.

File and Analyze the Residuals
The differences (suitably rescaled, see *BD Section 9.4*) between the observations and the corresponding one-step predictors are the residuals from the model. If the fitted model were the true model, they would constitute a white noise sequence. This allows us to check, by studying the residuals, whether or not the model is a good fit to the data. Further details of this option are given in Section 2.4.

Predict Future Data (and Return to Main Menu)
The fitted model can be used to compute best linear h-step predictors

```
THE ARMA( 0,25) MODEL IS  X(t) = Z(t)
+(  -.433)*Z(t- 1)  +(  -.305)*Z(t- 3)  +(   .238)*Z(t- 5)  +(  -.656)*Z(t-12)
+(   .351)*Z(t-23)

ESTIMATED MA COEFFICIENTS at lags  1  3  5 12 23
    -.433170           -.305410          .238279          -.655968           .350812
STANDARD ERRORS
     .101268            .078332          .086034           .080842           .092937

    <Press any key to continue>
```

FIGURE 2.15. *The standard errors of the coefficient estimators*

for both the transformed and original series. This option is also available
directly from the Main Menu and is discussed later in Section 2.6.

✓ Standard Errors of Estimated Coefficients

This option prints the standard errors (estimated standard deviations)
of the coefficient estimators on the screen. These standard errors are
evaluated by numerical determination of the Hessian matrix of $-2 \ln L$
(*BD Section 9.2*).

> EXAMPLE: Starting from the Results Menu, type **t** to display
> the standard errors for the coefficient estimators in the model,
> AIRPASS.MOD, just fitted to the logged, differenced and mean-
> corrected AIRPASS.DAT series (see Figure 2.15).

✓ Matrix of Correlations of the Estimated Coefficients

The estimated correlation matrix of the coefficient estimators can be
printed on the screen by typing **M**.

> EXAMPLE: Type **M** to obtain the estimated correlations for the
> coefficient estimators in the model for the logged, differenced
> and mean-corrected AIRPASS.DAT series (see Figure 2.16).

NON-INVERTIBLE MODEL. Switch to Invertible Model

If *PEST* fits a non-invertible (Section 2.6.1) ARMA(p, q) model to your

```
THE ARMA( 0,25) MODEL IS  X(t) = Z(t)
+(   -.433)*Z(t- 1)   +(  -.305)*Z(t- 3)   +(    .238)*Z(t- 5)   +(  -.656)*Z(t-12)
+(   .351)*Z(t-23)

ESTIMATED MA COEFFICIENTS at lags  1  3  5 12 23
        -.433170            -.305410            .238279           -.655968             .350812

CORRELATION MATRIX OF ESTIMATORS
 (Printed one row at a time; press any key to see the next row.)

.100E+01 -.420E+00 -.334E+00 -.102E+00 -.173E+00

-.420E+00  .100E+01 -.118E+00  .232E+00 -.368E+00

-.334E+00 -.118E+00  .100E+01 -.489E+00  .366E-01

-.102E+00  .232E+00 -.489E+00  .100E+01 -.393E+00

-.173E+00 -.368E+00  .366E-01 -.393E+00  .100E+01

    <Press any key to continue>
```

FIGURE 2.16. *The correlation matrix of the coefficient estimators*

data set, you can convert to an equivalent invertible ARMA(p, q) model by typing **N**. Equivalent here means from a second-order point of view. Note however that a non-invertible subset ARMA(p, q) model will generally convert to an invertible ARMA(p, q) model with all q moving average coefficients non-zero. Once the model is converted to an invertible model (if it is important to do so), Options **t** and **M** (for computing standard errors and correlations) disappear from the Results Menu. At this stage, one should reoptimize (type **C O**) with the invertible model to get the standard errors of the estimated parameters.

2.4 Testing Your Model (*BD Section 9.4*)

Once we have a model, it is important to check whether it is any good or not. Typically this is judged by comparing observations with corresponding predicted values obtained from the fitted model. If the fitted model is appropriate then the prediction errors should behave in a manner which is consistent with the model.

We define the **residuals** to be the rescaled one-step prediction errors,

$$\hat{W}_t = (X_t - \hat{X}_t)/\sqrt{r_{t-1}},$$

where $\hat{X}_t$ is the best linear mean-square predictor of X_t based on the ob-

```
RESIDUALS MENU:    File residuals
                   Plot rescaled residuals
                   ACF/PACF of residuals
                   File ACF/PACF of residuals
                   Tests of randomness of residuals
                   Return to display of estimation results
```

FIGURE 2.17. *The Residuals Menu*

servations up to time $t - 1$, $r_{t-1} = E(X_t - \hat{X}_t)^2/\sigma^2$ and σ^2 is the white noise variance of the fitted model.

If the data were truly generated by the fitted ARMA(p, q) model with white noise sequence $\{Z_t\}$, then for large samples the properties of $\{\hat{W}_t\}$ should reflect those of $\{Z_t\}$ (see *BD Section 9.4*). To check the appropriateness of the model we can therefore examine the residual series $\{\hat{W}_t\}$, and check that it resembles a realization of a white noise sequence.

PEST provides a number of tests for doing this in the Residuals Menu which is obtained by selecting the option [File and Analyze Residuals] of the Results Menu.

To examine the residuals from a *specified* model without doing any optimization, enter the data and model, then use the option [Likelihood of Model] of the Estimation Menu followed by [File and Analyze Residuals] of the Results Menu.

EXAMPLE: Type **F** while in the Results Menu and you will see the screen display shown in Figure 2.17.

2.4.1 PLOTTING THE RESIDUALS

The residuals $\hat{W}_t$, $t = 1, \ldots, n$ were defined in Section 2.4. The rescaled residuals are defined as

$$\hat{W}_t^{(r)} = \sqrt{n}\hat{W}_t / (\sum_{j=1}^{n} \hat{W}_t^2).$$

From the Residuals Menu type **P** and you will see a histogram of the rescaled residuals.

If the fitted model is appropriate, the histogram of the rescaled residuals should have mean close to zero. If the fitted model is appropriate and the data is Gaussian, this will be reflected in the shape of the histogram, which should then resemble a normal density with mean zero and variance one.

Press any key after inspecting the histogram and you will see a graph of $\hat{W}_t^{(r)}$ vs t. If the fitted model is appropriate this should resemble a realization of a white noise sequence. Look for trends, cycles and non-constant variance, any of which suggest that the fitted model is inappropriate. If substantially more than 5% of the rescaled residuals lie outside the bounds ± 1.96 or if there are rescaled residuals far outside these bounds, then the fitted model should not be regarded as Gaussian.

> EXAMPLE: After selecting the option [**Plot rescaled residuals**] of the Residuals Menu you will see the histogram of the rescaled residuals as shown in Figure 2.18. The mean is close to zero and the shape suggests that the assumption of Gaussian white noise is not unreasonable in our proposed model for the transformed airline passenger data.
>
> Press any key to see the graph shown in Figure 2.19. A few of the rescaled residuals are greater in magnitude than 1.96 (as is to be expected), but there are no obvious indications here that the model is inappropriate. Press any key then enter $\hookleftarrow$ and type **C** to return to the Residuals Menu.

2.4.2 ACF/PACF OF THE RESIDUALS (*BD Section 9.4*)

If we were to assume that our fitted model is the true process generating the data, then the observed residuals would be realized values of a white noise sequence. We can check the hypothesis that $\{W_t\}$ is an independent white noise sequence by examining the sample autocorrelations of the observed residuals which should resemble observations of independent normal random variables with mean 0 and variance $1/n$ (see *BD Example 7.2.1*).

In particular the sample ACF of the observed residuals should lie within the bounds $\pm 1.96/\sqrt{n}$ roughly 95% of the time. These bounds are displayed on the graphs of the ACF and PACF. If substantially more than 5% of the

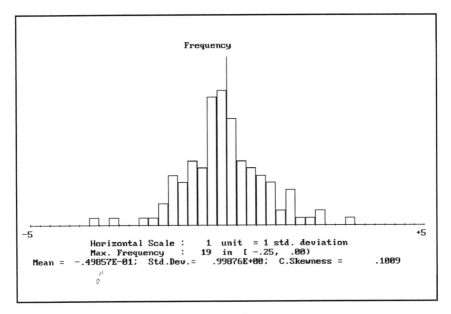

FIGURE 2.18. *Histogram of the rescaled residuals from AIRPASS.MOD*

correlations are outside these limits, or if there are a few very large values, then we should look for a better-fitting model. (More precise bounds, due to Box and Pierce, can be found in *BD Section 9.4.*)

> EXAMPLE: Choose the option [ACF/PACF of residuals] of the Residuals Menu. After entering ↩ , the sample ACF and PACF of the residuals will then appear as shown in Figure 2.20. No correlations are outside the bounds in this case. They appear to be compatible with the hypothesis that the residuals are in fact observations of a white noise sequence. Type ↩ to return to the Residuals Menu.

2.4.3 TESTING FOR RANDOMNESS OF THE RESIDUALS (*BD Section 9.4*)

The option [Tests of randomness of the residuals] in the Residuals Menu provides six tests of the hypothesis that the residuals are observations from an independent and identically distributed (iid) sequence.

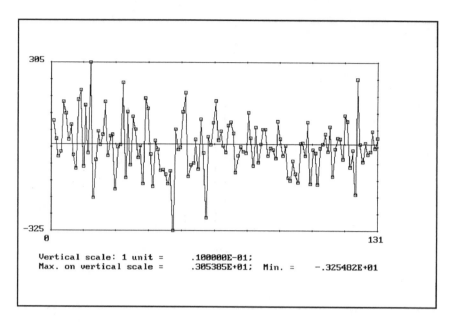

FIGURE 2.19. *Time plot of the rescaled residuals from AIRPASS.MOD*

THE LJUNG-BOX PORTMANTEAU TEST

This test, due to Ljung and Box, pools the sample autocorrelations of the residuals instead of looking at them individually. The statistic used is

$$Q = n(n+2) \sum_{k=1}^{h} \hat{\rho}_W^2(k)/(n-k),$$

where $\hat{\rho}_W(k)$ is the sample autocorrelation of the residuals at lag k, and h is to be specified. As a rule of thumb, h should be of the order of $\sqrt{n}$, where n is the sample size ($h=20$ is a commonly used value).

If the data had in fact been generated by the fitted ARMA(p,q) model, then for large n, Q would have an approximate χ^2 distribution with $h-p-q$ degrees of freedom. The test rejects the proposed model at level α if the observed value of Q is larger than the $(1-\alpha)$ quantile of the χ^2_{h-p-q} distribution.

This test frequently fails to reject poorly fitting models. Care should be taken not to accept a model on the basis of the portmanteau test alone.

THE MCLEOD-LI PORTMANTEAU TEST

This test is used for testing the hypothesis that the residuals are observations from an iid sequence of normally distributed random variables. It is based on the same statistic used for the Ljung-Box test, except that the

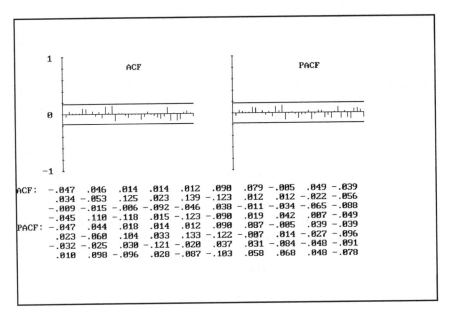

FIGURE 2.20. *ACF/PACF of the residuals from AIRPASS.MOD*

sample autocorrelations of the residuals, $\hat{\rho}_W(h)$, are replaced by the sample autocorrelations of the "squared" residuals, $\hat{\rho}_{WW}(h)$, giving

$$\tilde{Q} = n(n+2) \sum_{k=1}^{h} \hat{\rho}_{WW}^2(k)/(n-k).$$

The hypothesis of iid normal residuals is then rejected at level α if the observed value of $\tilde{Q}$ is larger than the $(1-\alpha)$ quantile of the χ_{h-p-q}^2 distribution.

A TEST BASED ON TURNING POINTS

The statistic, T, used in this test is the number of turning points in the sequence of residuals. It can be shown that for an iid sequence, T is asymptotically normal with mean $\mu_T = 2(n-2)/3$ and variance $\sigma_T^2 = (16n-29)/90$.

The hypothesis that the residuals constitute a sequence of iid observations is rejected if

$$|T - \mu_T|/\sigma_T > \Phi_{1-\alpha/2},$$

where $\Phi_{1-\alpha/2}$ is the $(1-\alpha/2)$ quantile of the standard normal distribution.

THE DIFFERENCE-SIGN TEST

Let S be the number of times the differenced residual series $\hat{W}_t - \hat{W}_{t-1}$ is positive. If $\{\hat{W}_t\}$ is an iid sequence it can be shown that S is asymptotically normal with mean $\mu_S = \frac{1}{2}(n-1)$ and variance $\sigma_S^2 = (n+1)/12$.

The hypothesis that the residuals constitute a sequence of iid observations is rejected if

$$|S - \mu_S|/\sigma_S > \Phi_{1-\alpha/2}.$$

This test must be used with caution. If the residuals have a strong cyclic component they will be likely to pass the difference-sign test since roughly half of the differences will be positive.

THE RANK TEST

This test is particularly useful for detecting a linear trend in the residuals. Let P be the number of pairs (i, j) such that $\hat{W}_j > \hat{W}_i$, and $j > i$, $i = 1, \ldots, n-1$. If the residuals are iid, the mean of P is $\mu_P = \frac{1}{4}n(n-1)$, the variance of P is $\sigma_P^2 = n(n-1)(2n+5)/8$ and P is asymptotically normal. The hypothesis that the residuals constitute a sequence of iid observations is rejected if

$$|P - \mu_P|/\sigma_P > \Phi_{1-\alpha/2}.$$

THE MINIMUM-AICC AR MODEL

If the residuals are compatible with a sequence of iid observations, then the minimum AICC autoregression fitted to the residuals should have order $p = 0$. *PEST* computes the AICC values for AR models of orders $0, 1, \ldots, 26$ fitted to the residuals using the Yule-Walker equations, after which the order p of the model with minimum-AICC value is displayed on the screen. A value of $p \geq 1$ suggests that some correlation remains in the residuals, contradicting the hypothesis that the residuals are observations from a white noise sequence.

> EXAMPLE: Type **T** from the Residuals Menu to test the residuals for randomness. You will then be prompted to input the value of h, the total number of sample autocorrelations of the residuals used to compute the Portmanteau statistics. After entering the suggested value of h (in this case *PEST* suggests using $h = 25$), the results of the six tests of randomness described above are shown in Figure 2.21. Every test is easily passed by our fitted model with $\alpha < .05$. Observe that the order of the minimum-AICC AR model for the residuals is $p = 0$. Press ↵ to return to the Residuals Menu. For later use, save the residuals under the filename AIRRES.DAT using the option [File residuals].

```
RANDOMNESS TEST STATISTICS (see section 9.4)
---------------------------------------------------------

LJUNG-BOX PORTM. =    13.76 CHISQUR(            20)

MCLEOD-LI PORTM. =    17.37 CHISQUR(            20)

TURNING POINTS   =      87. ANORMAL(    86.00         4.79**2)

DIFFERENCE-SIGN  =      65. ANORMAL(    65.00         3.32**2)

RANK TEST        =    3935. ANORMAL(  4257.50       753.91**2)

ORDER OF MIN AICC YW MODEL FOR RESIDUALS =    0


   <Press any key to continue>
```

FIGURE 2.21. *Tests of randomness for the residuals from AIRPASS.MOD*

2.5   Prediction (*BD Chapter 5, Section 9.5*)

One of the main purposes of time series modelling is the prediction of future observations. Once you have found a suitable model for your data, you can predict future values using either the option [**Forecasting**] of the Main Menu or (equivalently) the option [**Predict Future Data**] of the Results Menu.

2.5.1   FORECAST CRITERIA

Given observations $X_1, \ldots, X_n$ of a series which we assume to be appropriately modelled as an ARMA(p, q) process, *PEST* predicts future values of the series X_{n+h} from the data and the model by computing the linear combination $P_n(X_{n+h})$ of $X_1, \ldots, X_n$ which minimizes the mean squared error $E(X_{n+h} - P_n(X_{n+h}))^2$.

2.5.2   FORECAST RESULTS

Assuming that you have data stored in *PEST* which has been adequately fitted by an ARMA(p, q) model, also stored in *PEST*, choose [**Forecasting**] from the Main Menu, after which you will be asked for the number of future values you wish to predict.

After the model is displayed on the screen you will be asked if you wish to change the white noise variance. (This will not affect the predictors but only their mean squared errors.) The predicted values of the fitted ARMA process will then be displayed in the column labelled XHAT. In the column labelled SQRT(MSE) you will see the square roots of the estimated mean squared errors of the corresponding predictors. These are calculated under the assumption that the observations are truly generated by the current model. They measure the uncertainty of the corresponding forecasts. A smaller value indicates a more reliable forecast. As is to be expected, the mean squared error of $P_n(X_{n+h})$ increases with the lead time h of the forecast.

Approximate 95% prediction bounds (*BD Section 5.4*) can be obtained from each predicted value by adding and subtracting $1.96\sqrt{MSE}$. These are exact under the assumptions that the model is Gaussian and faithfully represents the data. They should not be interpreted as 95% bounds if the histogram of the residuals is decidedly non-Gaussian in appearance.

If your data was mean-corrected, the third column of the *PEST* output will show the predicted values in Column 1 plus the previously subtracted sample mean. If there has been no mean-correction, the third column will be the same as the first.

2.5.3 INVERTING TRANSFORMATIONS

The predictors and mean squared errors calculated so far do not pertain to your *original* time series unless you have made no data transformations other than mean-correction (in which case the relevant predictors are those in the third column). What we have found are predictors of your *transformed* series. To predict the original series, you will need to invert all the data transformations which you have made in order to fit a zero-mean stationary model. *PEST* will do this for you. In fact one transformation, mean-correction, has already been inverted to generate the predicted values which were displayed in Column 3.

If you used differencing transformations, you will see the Prediction Menu displayed following the printing of the ARMA predictors. Type U to select the option [Undo differencing]. The predictors of the undifferenced data (still Box-Coxed if you made such a transformation) will then be printed on the screen together with the square roots of their mean squared errors. Type ↔ and the undifferenced data will be plotted. Type ↔ again and the predicted values will be added to the graph of the data. Type C and you will be asked if you wish to invert the Box-Cox transformation (if you made one). If so type Y and the original data will be plotted on the screen. Type ↔ again and the predictors of the original series will be added to the graph. Type C and you will be asked if you wish to file the predicted values, then returned to the Prediction Menu.

If you used classical decomposition rather than differencing, *PEST* will automatically add back the trend and/or seasonal component immediately

#	XHAT	SQRT(MSE)	XHAT+MEAN (=	.29088E-03)
132	.102745E-01	.342159E-01	.105654E-01	
133	.869003E-02	.363938E-01	.898091E-02	
134	.390377E-01	.363936E-01	.393286E-01	
135	-.401249E-01	.374919E-01	-.398340E-01	
136	-.126029E-01	.375666E-01	-.123120E-01	
137	.892824E-02	.379380E-01	.921912E-02	
138	.698649E-03	.379463E-01	.989527E-03	
139	.913227E-02	.380124E-01	.942314E-02	
140	-.179913E-02	.380406E-01	-.150826E-02	
141	.220069E-02	.380461E-01	.249156E-02	
142	.139082E-01	.380449E-01	.141990E-01	
143	-.151046E-01	.380461E-01	-.148137E-01	
144	-.203344E-02	.427621E-01	-.174256E-02	
145	-.214808E-01	.427639E-01	-.211900E-01	
146	.256439E-01	.427640E-01	.259348E-01	
147	.103776E-02	.427759E-01	.132864E-02	
148	-.636410E-02	.427885E-01	-.607322E-02	
149	.761748E-03	.427923E-01	.105263E-02	
150	-.386886E-02	.428007E-01	-.357798E-02	
151	-.343099E-02	.428021E-01	-.314011E-02	

⟨Press any key to continue⟩

FIGURE 2.22. *Prediction of the transformed series, AIRPASS.DAT*

after listing the ARMA predictors. The resulting data values and corresponding predictors will then be plotted, after which you will again be given the opportunity to invert the Box-Cox transformation (if any) as in the previous paragraph.

EXAMPLE: We left our logged, differenced and mean-corrected airline passenger data stored in *PEST* as AIRPASS.DAT along with the fitted MA(23) model, AIRPASS.MOD. To predict the next 24 values of the original series AIRPASS.DAT, return to the Main Menu and select the option [Forecasting]. Type 24↩ to specify that 24 predicted values are required after the last observation. After a brief delay and a ↩ , you will be asked if you wish to change the white noise variance. Type N and the predictors will be displayed as in Figure 2.22. (Only the first 11 predicted points are shown.)

To obtain forecasts of the undifferenced series, choose the option [Undo differencing] from the Prediction Menu and follow the program prompts to obtain the graph shown in Figure 2.23. Here the hollow squares represent the observations and the solid squares represent the forecast values. Notice how the model has captured the regular cyclic behaviour in the data.

To undo the Box-Cox transformation and recover the original data and predictors, type ↩ C Y ↩ and a graph of the

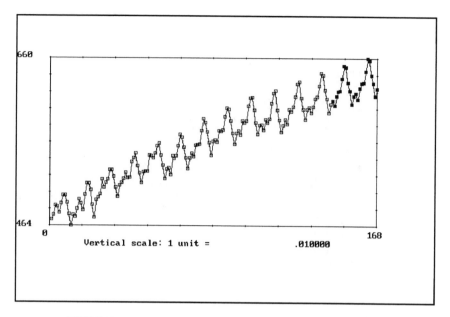

FIGURE 2.23. *The forecast values with differencing inverted*

original AIRPASS data will be plotted on the screen. Type ↩
and the 24 predicted values will be added, giving the graph
shown in Figure 2.24.

2.6 Model Properties

PEST can be used to analyze the properties of a specified ARMA process
without reference to any data set. This enables us in particular to compare
the properties of potential ARMA models for a given data set in order to
see which of them best reproduces particular features of the data.

  PEST allows you to look at the autocorrelation function and spectral
density, to examine $MA(\infty)$ and $AR(\infty)$ representations and to generate
realizations for any specified ARMA process. The use of these options is
described in this section.

  EXAMPLE: We shall illustrate the use of *PEST* for model analysis using the model AIRPASS.MOD which is currently stored
  in the program.

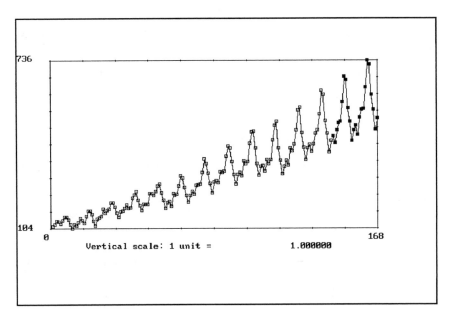

FIGURE 2.24. *The forecasts of the original AIRPASS data*

2.6.1   ARMA MODELS (*BD Chapter 3*)

For modelling zero-mean stationary time series, *PEST* uses the class of ARMA processes. The initials stand for **A**uto**R**egressive **M**oving **A**verage. *PEST* enables you to compute characteristics of specific ARMA models and to find appropriate models for given data sets (assuming of course that the data can be reasonably represented by such a model — preliminary transformations of the data may be necessary to ensure this).

$\{X_t\}$ is an ARMA(p, q) process with coefficients $\phi_1, \ldots, \phi_p, \theta_1, \ldots, \theta_q$ and white noise variance σ^2 if it is a stationary solution of the difference equations,

$$X_t = \phi_1 X_{t-1} + \phi_2 X_{t-2} + \cdots + \phi_p X_{t-p} + Z_t + \theta_1 Z_{t-1} + \theta_2 Z_{t-2} + \cdots + \theta_q Z_{t-q},$$

where $\{Z_t\} \sim \mathrm{WN}(0, \sigma^2)$ (i.e. $\{Z_t\}$ is an uncorrelated sequence of random variables with mean 0 and variance σ^2, known as a **white-noise sequence**.)

If $p = 0$ we call X_t an MA(q) (moving average of order q) process. In this case,

$$X_t = Z_t + \theta_1 Z_{t-1} + \theta_2 Z_{t-2} + \cdots + \theta_q Z_{t-q}.$$

If $q = 0$ we call X_t an AR(p) (autoregressive of order p) process. In this case,

$$X_t = Z_t + \phi_1 X_{t-1} + \phi_2 X_{t-2} + \cdots + \phi_p X_{t-p}.$$

An ARMA model is said to be **causal** if X_t has the MA(∞) representation in terms of $\{Z_t\}$,

$$X_t = \sum_{j=0}^{\infty} \psi_j Z_{t-j}, \quad t = 0, \pm 1, \pm 2, \ldots,$$

where $\sum_{j=0}^{\infty} |\psi_j| < \infty$ and $\psi_0 := 1$. If the **AR polynomial**, $1 - \phi_1 z - \cdots - \phi_p z^p$, and the **MA polynomial**, $1 + \theta_1 z + \cdots + \theta_p z^q$, have no common zeroes, then a necessary and sufficient condition for causality is that the autoregressive polynomial has no zeroes inside or on the unit circle.

PEST works exclusively with causal ARMA models. It will not permit you to enter a model for which $1 - \phi_1 z - \cdots - \phi_p z^p$ has a zero inside or on the unit circle, nor does it generate fitted models with this property. From the point of view of second order properties this represents no loss of generality (*BD Section 3.1*). If you are trying to enter an ARMA(p, q) model manually, the simplest way to ensure that your model is causal is to set all the autoregressive coefficients close to zero (e.g. .001). *PEST* will not accept a non-causal model.

An ARMA model is said to be **invertible** if Z_t can be written as

$$Z_t = \sum_{j=0}^{\infty} \pi_j X_{t-j}, \quad t = 0, \pm 1, \pm 2, \ldots,$$

where $\sum_{j=0}^{\infty} |\pi_j| < \infty$ and $\pi_0 := 1$. This condition ensures that Z_t, the noise at time t, is determined by the observations at times up to and including t, or equivalently that $\{X_t\}$ has an "AR(∞)" representation in terms of $\{Z_t\}$.

PEST does not restrict models to be invertible, however if the current model is non-invertible, i.e. if the moving average polynomial, $1 + \theta_1 z + \cdots + \theta_q z^q$ has a zero inside or on the unit circle, you will be informed by the program. (You can check the model status by choosing the option [Current model and data file status] of the Main Menu.) A non-invertible model can always be converted to an invertible model with the same auto-covariance function by choosing [ARMA parameter estimation] of the Main Menu, then option [Likelihood of Model] of the Estimation Menu, then option [NONINVERTIBLE MODEL] from the Results Menu.

2.6.2 Model ACF, PACF (*BD Sections 3.3, 3.4*)

See Section 2.3.1 for a definition of the ACF and PACF and the use of the sample ACF and PACF in model fitting.

The *model* ACF and PACF can be obtained using the selection [**Model ACF/PACF, AR/MA infinity representations**] of the Main Menu. They can be calculated for lags up to 1150. Normally you should not need more than about 40.

After typing **M** from the Main Menu, the Model ACF/PACF Menu consisting of 7 items will appear. It allows you to reset the maximum lag (the default value is 40), to plot the ACF and PACF, to file the values, to plot the sample ACF and PACF with the model ACF and PACF, to change the white noise variance and to compute the coefficients in the MA(∞) and AR(∞) representations of the process (see Section 2.6.3).

> EXAMPLE: Starting from the Main Menu, the ACF and PACF for the current model AIRPASS.MOD may be plotted by typing **M A**. To compare the sample ACF/PACF with the model ACF/PACF, press ↩ to return to the Model ACF/PACF Menu and type **S**. The graphs are shown in Figure 2.25. The vertical lines represent the model ACF/PACF and the solid black squares correspond to the sample ACF/PACF. These graphs show that the data and the model ACF and PACF all have large values at lag 12 while the sample and model partial autocorrelation functions both tend to die away geometrically after the peak at lag 12. The similarities between the graphs indicate that the model is capturing some of the important features of the data.

2.6.3   MODEL REPRESENTATIONS (*BD Sections 3.1, 3.2*)

As indicated in Section 2.6.1, if $\{X_t\}$ is a causal ARMA process, then it has as an MA(∞) representation,

$$X_t = \sum_{j=0}^{\infty} \psi_j Z_{t-j}, \quad t = 0, \pm 1, \pm 2, \ldots,$$

where $\sum_{j=0}^{\infty} |\psi_j| < \infty$ and $\psi_0 = 1$.

Similarly, if $\{X_t\}$ is an invertible ARMA process, then it has an AR(∞) representation,

$$Z_t = \sum_{j=0}^{\infty} \pi_j X_{t-j}, \quad t = 0, \pm 1, \pm 2, \ldots,$$

where $\sum_{j=0}^{\infty} |\pi_j| < \infty$ and $\pi_0 = 1$.

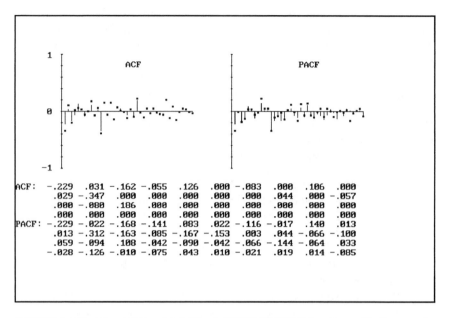

ACF: -.229   .031 -.162 -.055   .126   .000 -.083   .000   .106   .000
       .029 -.347   .000   .000   .000   .000   .000   .044   .000 -.057
       .000 -.080   .186   .000   .000   .000   .000   .000   .000   .000
       .000   .000   .000   .000   .000   .000   .000   .000   .000   .000
PACF: -.229 -.022 -.168 -.141   .083   .022 -.116 -.017   .140   .013
       .013 -.312 -.163 -.085 -.167 -.153   .003   .044 -.066 -.100
       .059 -.094   .108 -.042 -.090 -.042 -.066 -.144 -.064   .033
      -.028 -.126 -.010 -.075   .043   .010 -.021   .019   .014 -.085

FIGURE 2.25. *The ACF and PACF of AIRPASS.MOD together with the sample ACF and PACF of the transformed AIRPASS.DAT series*

For any specified ARMA model you can determine the coefficients in these representations by selecting the option [MA or AR infinity representations] from the Model ACF/PACF Menu. Starting from the Main Menu type **M M.** You will then be asked to choose between the [MA-Infinity Representation] and [AR-Infinity Representation] of the model. (If the model is not invertible the $AR(\infty)$ choice will not be possible.) After entering the maximum lag required, *PEST* will then print the desired coefficients (ψ_j or π_j) on the screen. They can be stored either as they appear on the screen or in model format for later use in *PEST* .

EXAMPLE: AIRPASS.MOD does not have an $AR(\infty)$ representation since it is not invertible. However, we can convert AIR-PASS.MOD to an equivalent invertible model and then find an $AR(\infty)$ representation for it. To convert to an invertible model, start from the Main Menu and type $\mathbf{A} \hookleftarrow \mathbf{L} \hookleftarrow \hookleftarrow \mathbf{N} \hookleftarrow \hookleftarrow \mathbf{R}.$ To find the $AR(\infty)$ representation, type **M M A** 50$\hookleftarrow$. This gives 50 coefficients, the first 19 of which are shown in Figure 2.26. There is little point in using *PEST* to find the $MA(\infty)$ representation of this model. What is it?

```
See Section 3.2 for notation

AR-infinity coeffs up to lag    50
       j          pi (j)
       0       1.0000000
       1        .3613552
       2        .1173539
       3        .3052557
       4        .2738022
       5       -.0051080
       6        .0538636
       7        .1687211
       8        .1005408
       9        .0208243
      10        .0813016
      11        .0672451
      12        .5841435
      13        .4196690
      14        .2307828
      15        .3741191
      16        .3943860
      17        .1059944
      18        .0887224
      19        .2328299
<Press any key to continue>
```

FIGURE 2.26. *The AR(∞) representation of the invertible equivalent of AIR-PASS.MOD*

2.6.4 GENERATING REALIZATIONS OF A RANDOM SERIES (*BD Problem 8.17*)

PEST can be used to generate realizations of a random time series defined by the currently stored model.

To generate such a realization, select the option [Generation of simulated data] from the Main Menu. You will be asked if you wish to continue with the simulation (type **Y**) and if you wish to change the white noise variance. Next you will be prompted for the number of data points you wish to generate and then you will be asked to enter a random number seed. This should be an integer with fewer than 10 digits. By using the same random number seed you can reproduce the same realization of the process at any other time.

Once the values of an ARMA process have been generated, you will be given the opportunity to add any specified mean to the observations. If you have previously mean-corrected a data set, the subtracted mean will have been stored by *PEST* and it will be displayed so that you may choose to add this value to the simulated ARMA data. (If you have previously performed a classical decomposition on a data set you will also be given the opportunity to add the stored trend and seasonal components. This allows you to simulate the *original data*, not just the random noise component. If, however, you transform your original data by differencing, *PEST* allows

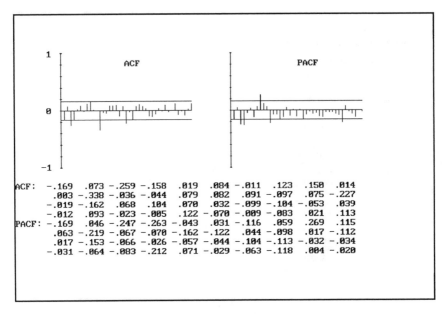

FIGURE 2.27. *The sample ACF and PACF of the generated data*

you to simulate the differenced data only.)

The simulated data will be stored in *PEST*, overwriting any data previously stored in the program.

> EXAMPLE: To generate 135 data points using the model AIR-
> PASS.MOD, type **G** from the Main Menu. Then type
> **G Y N** 135↵ 1327↵ 0↵ **N**

> (The number 1327 is the random number seed.) Plot the sample
> ACF and PACF of the generated data using Option 3 of the
> Data Menu (see Figure 2.27). Compare the graphs with those
> in Figure 2.25. By computing the sample ACF and PACF for
> a variety of different realizations you can get a feeling for the
> magnitude of the random fluctuations in these functions.

> The sample ACF and PACF of the transformed airline passen-
> ger data (Figure 2.9) look equally compatible with the model
> ACF and PACF (Figure 2.25) as the sample ACF and PACF
> of the simulated series. This reinforces our earlier decision that
> the model provides a good representation of the data.

2.6.5   MODEL SPECTRAL DENSITY (*BD Sections 4.1–4.4*)

Just as we compared the sample ACF and PACF of the data with the ACF
and PACF of the fitted model, we can compare the estimated spectral

SPECTRAL DENSITY MENU:

```
Spectral density
File the spectral density
ln(spectral density)
File ln(spectral density)
New value for n
Change white noise variance
Return to main menu
```

FIGURE 2.28. *The Spectral Density Menu*

density based on the data with the spectral density of the model. Spectral density estimation is treated in Section 2.7. Here we consider only the spectral density of the *model*. This is determined by selecting the option [Spectral density of MODEL on (-pi,pi)] of the Main Menu. The Spectral Density Menu is shown in Figure 2.28.

The spectral density of a stationary time series $\{X_t,\ t = 0 \pm 1, \cdots\}$ with absolutely summable autocovariances (in particular of an ARMA process) can be written as

$$f(\omega) = \frac{1}{2\pi} \sum_{k=-\infty}^{\infty} \gamma(k)e^{-i\omega k}, \quad -\pi \leq \omega \leq \pi,$$

where $\gamma(k)$ is the autocovariance at lag k and $i = \sqrt{-1}$.

The spectral representation of X_t decomposes the sequence into sinusoidal components and $f(\omega)$ measures the relative contributions to the variance of X_t from the components of different frequencies (measured in radians per unit time). For real-valued series $f(\omega) = f(-\omega)$ so it is necessary only to plot $f(\omega)$, $0 \leq \omega \leq \pi$. A peak in the spectral density function at frequency λ indicates a relatively large contribution to the variance from frequencies near λ.

For example the maximum likelihood AR(2) model,

$$X_t = 1.407X_{t-1} - 0.713X_{t-2} + Z_t,$$

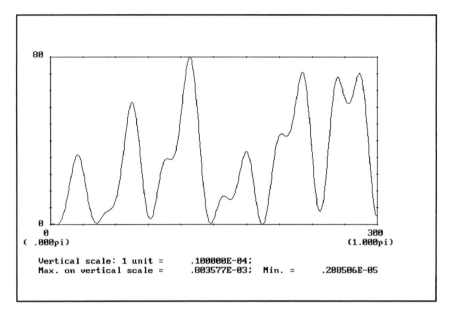

FIGURE 2.29. *The spectral density of AIRPASS.MOD*

for the data file SUNSPOTS.DAT has a peak in the spectral density at frequency $.18\pi$ radians per year. This indicates that a relatively large part of the variance of the series can be attributed to sinusoidal components with period close to $2\pi/(.18\pi) = 11.2$ years.

> EXAMPLE: To plot the spectral density of AIRPASS.MOD, start from the Main Menu and type $S \hookleftarrow S$. You will then see the graph displayed in Figure 2.29. A notable feature of this graph is that there are small values at each integer multiple of $\pi/6$. These are due to our earlier differencing at lag 12 which had the effect of removing period 12 components from the data.

The other options in the Spectral Density Menu allow you to file the spectral density, and to plot and file the logarithm of the spectral density. You can change the resolution of the spectral density graph using the option [New value for n]. The option [Change white noise variance] allows you specify a new white noise variance for the model.

```
Number of observations=    131

<Computing the Fourier transform>

SPECTRAL ANALYSIS MENU :

    Periodogram/(2*pi) and its logarithm
    Cumulative periodogram (normalized)
    File Fourier transform
    Apply Fisher's test
    Enter weights for spectral window
    Periodogram/(2*pi) with MODEL spectrum
    Cumulative periodogram with MODEL analogue
    Return to main menu
```

FIGURE 2.30. *The Spectral Analysis Menu*

2.7 Nonparametric Spectral Estimation (*BD Chapter 10*)

Spectral analysis is typically concerned with two problems: the detection of cyclical behavior in the data and the estimation of the spectral density. Both of these problems may be addressed by selecting [**Nonparametric spectral estimation**] from the Main Menu of *PEST*. After choosing this option, the Spectral Analysis Menu (see Figure 2.30) will appear on the screen.

2.7.1 PLOTTING THE PERIODOGRAM

The periodogram and/or ln(periodogram) may be plotted by choosing [**Plot periodogram/(2*pi) and its logarithm**] of the menu. The periodogram is defined by

$$I(\omega_j) = n^{-1}|\sum_{t=1}^{n} X_t e^{-it\omega_j}|^2$$

where $\omega_j = 2\pi j/n$, $j = 0, 1, \ldots, [n/2]$ are the Fourier frequencies in $[0, \pi]$ and $[n/2]$ is the integer part of $n/2$. (The program actually plots the rescaled periodogram $I(\omega_j)/(2\pi)$.) A large value of $I(\omega_j)$ suggests the presence of a sinusoidal component in the data at frequency ω_j. The presence of such a component may be tested using an analysis of variance table as described in *BD Section 10.1*. Alternatively, one can test for hidden periodicities in the data using the Kolmogorov–Smirnov test or Fisher's test as described below. The periodogram is computed for nonzero Fourier frequencies only, since the value at 0, $I(0) = n|\bar{X}_n|^2$, depends on the sample mean only and is generally not a useful quantity. The periodogram is computed using the fast Fourier transform. The discrete Fourier transform of the data, defined by

$$a_j = n^{-1/2} \sum_{t=1}^{n} X_t e^{-it\omega_j}, \quad -[(n-1)/2] \le j \le [n/2],$$

may be filed using the option [**File Fourier transform**]. This option will save the coefficients $\{a_j, j = 0, \ldots, [n/2]\}$ as an array of complex numbers.

EXAMPLE: Read in the stored data file AIRPASS.DAT, take logarithms, difference at lags 12 and 1 and then subtract the mean. From the Main Menu, type **N P** to plot the periodogram divided by (2π). The option [**Periodogram/(2∗pi) with MODEL spectrum**] overlays the model spectral density with $1/(2\pi)$ times the periodogram of the data. To choose this option, press ↩ to return to the Spectral Analysis Menu, then type **E** to obtain the graphs shown in Figure 2.31. Notice the similarity between them. Now return to the Main Menu and read in the residuals AIRRES.DAT which we filed earlier after fitting AIRPASS.MOD to the transformed AIRPASS.DAT series. To check the compatibility of the residuals with white noise, enter a white noise model with variance .0010277 (the sample variance of AIRRES.DAT) using the option [**Entry of an ARMA(p,q) model**] in the Main Menu. (Starting from the Main Menu, the necessary keystrokes to enter this model are **E** 0↩ 0↩ ↩ **A** .0010277 ↩ ↩ **R**.)

Now if we type **N E** to compute the periodogram/(2π) and overlay it with the current model spectrum (which is constant), we see (Figure 2.32) that there are no dominant frequency components, so that in this respect the residual series resembles a realization of white noise. For an iid sequence with variance σ^2 the periodogram ordinates should be approximately iid exponential variables with mean σ^2.

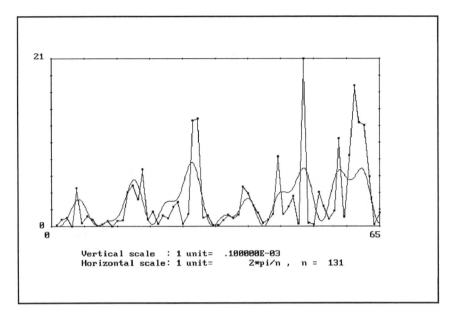

FIGURE 2.31. *Periodogram of the logged and twice differenced AIRPASS.DAT series*

2.7.2 PLOTTING THE CUMULATIVE PERIODOGRAM

Select [**Cumulative periodogram (normalized)**] from the Spectral Analysis Menu to plot the standardized cumulative periodogram defined as

$$C(x) = \begin{cases} 0, & x < 1 \\ Y_i, & i \le x < i+1, \, i = 1, \ldots, q-1, \\ 1, & x \ge q, \end{cases}$$

where $q = [(n-1)/2]$ and

$$Y_i = \frac{\sum_{k=1}^{i} I(\omega_k)}{\sum_{k=1}^{q} I(\omega_k)}.$$

If $\{X_t\}$ is Gaussian white noise, then $Y_i, i = 1, \ldots, q-1$ are distributed as the order statistics from a sample of $q-1$ independent uniform(0,1) random variables, and the standardized cumulative periodogram should be approximately linear. The hypothesis of Gaussian white noise is rejected at level .05 if $C(x)$ exits from the boundaries

$$y = \frac{x-1}{q-1} \pm 1.36(q-1)^{-1/2}, \quad 1 \le x \le q.$$

EXAMPLE: After returning to the Spectral Analysis Menu, type **U** to plot the standardized cumulative periodogram with the

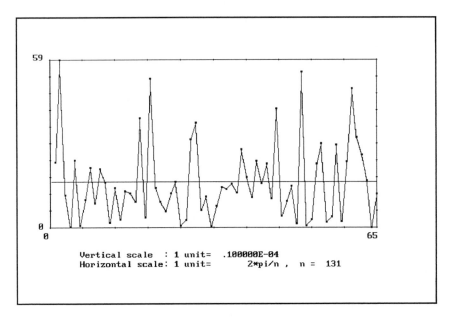

Vertical scale : 1 unit= .100000E-04
Horizontal scale: 1 unit=   2*pi/n , n = 131

FIGURE 2.32. *Periodogram of the residuals from AIRPASS.DAT*

model analogue (Figure 2.33) for AIRRES.DAT. Since the current model in *PEST* is white noise the model analogue will be a straight line. As can be seen from the figure, the function $C(x)$ lies well within the above boundaries (here $q = [(131 - 1)/2] = 65$), supporting the hypothesis that the residuals are observations of independent white noise.

2.7.3   FISHER'S TEST

Fisher's test enables you to test the data for the presence of hidden periodicities with unspecified frequency. If the test statistic defined by

$$\xi_q = \frac{\max_{1 \le i \le q} I(\omega_i)}{q^{-1} \sum_{i=1}^{q} I(\omega_i)}$$

is large then the hypothesis that the data is Gaussian white noise is rejected. The option [**Apply Fisher's test**] of the Spectral Analysis Menu gives the observed value of ξ_q and the *p*-value of the test (i.e. the probability that ξ_q exceeds the observed value under the null hypothesis that the data is Gaussian white noise).

EXAMPLE: To apply Fisher's test to AIRRES.DAT, type **A** starting from the Spectral Analysis Menu and you will see the

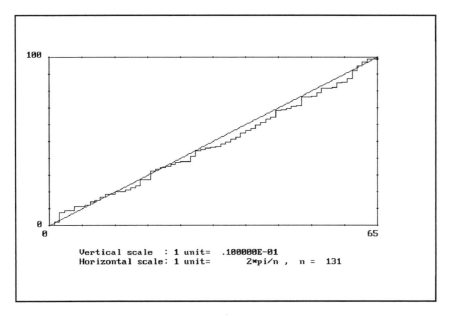

Vertical scale : 1 unit= .100000E-01
Horizontal scale: 1 unit=   2*pi/n , n = 131

FIGURE 2.33. *Cumulative periodogram of the residuals*

display,

```
Observed ratio of maximum periodogram to average  =    3.5954
Probability (under Ho) of ratio larger than observed = 0.8840
```

Since the p-value is rather large, Fisher's test does not suggest rejecting the hypothesis of iid residuals.

2.7.4   SMOOTHING TO ESTIMATE THE SPECTRAL DENSITY (*BD Section 10.4*)

The spectral density of a stationary process is estimated by smoothing the periodogram. The weight function $\{W(j), |j| \leq m\}$ used for smoothing is entered through the selection [Enter weights for spectral window] of the menu. After typing N, you will be asked to enter a value for m. Type $-1\hookleftarrow$ if a weight function is to be read from a file and type $0\hookleftarrow$ if you want to return to the Spectral Analysis Menu. For positive values of m you will be requested to enter the weights $W(0), W(1), \ldots, W(m)$, all of which must be nonnegative. The program ensures that the weight function is symmetric by defining $W(-j) = W(j), j = 1, \ldots, m$, and then rescales the weights so that they add to one. After the weights have been entered, the program returns to the Spectral Analysis Menu which now contains the 3 new items, [Weight function (plot and file)], [Spectrum density estimate (windowed)], and [Windowed spectral estimate with MODEL spectrum].

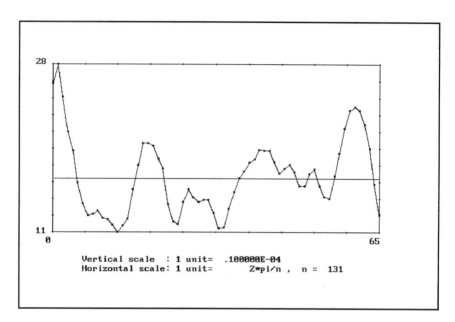

FIGURE 2.34. *Smoothed spectrum estimate for AIRRES.DAT*

EXAMPLE: Try estimating the spectral density of the data file AIRRES.DAT using the weight function, $W(0) = W(1) = W(2) = \frac{3}{21}, W(3) = \frac{2}{21}$, and $W(4) = \frac{1}{21}$. Begin by typing **N** 4↩ 3↩ 3↩ 3↩ 2↩ 1↩ . (The program automatically divides the weights entered by 21 so that they add to 1). Plot the weight function by typing **W**. The entries ↩ **C N** return you to the Spectral Analysis Menu. Type **I**↩ to plot the smoothed periodogram together with the model spectral density (Figure 2.34). This can be plotted on a more natural scale by typing ↩ **R**↩ .0003↩ 0↩ (see Figure 2.35). Approximate 95% confidence bounds for the true spectral density, $f(\omega_j)$, are given (*BD* Section 10.4) by,

$$\hat{f}(\omega_j) \pm 1.96 \left(\sum_{|k| \leq m} W^2(k) \right)^{1/2} \hat{f}(\omega_j) \quad \text{or}$$
$$\hat{f}(\omega_j) \pm .6921 \hat{f}(\omega_j)$$

These bounds are compatible with the constant spectral density of white noise.

The estimate $\ln \hat{f}$ of the ln[spectrum] can be plotted by typing ↩ **C N Y**. Approximate 95% confidence bounds for $\ln f(\omega_j)$

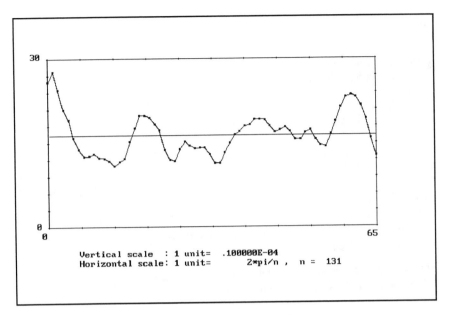

FIGURE 2.35. *Rescaled spectrum estimate for AIRRES.DAT*

are given by

$$\ln \hat{f}(\omega_j) \quad \pm \quad 1.96 \left(\sum_{|k| \le m} W^2(k) \right)^{1/2} \quad \text{or}$$
$$\ln \hat{f}(\omega_j) \quad \pm \quad .6921$$

It is often more convenient to make inferences for $\ln f$ since the widths of the confidence intervals are the same for all frequencies.

3

SMOOTH

3.1 Introduction (*BD Section 1.4*)

To run the program *SMOOTH*, double click on the icon labelled *smooth* from the *itsmw* window (or in DOS type SMOOTH from the C:\ITSMW directory). After pressing ↵ to clear the screen of the title page, you will be asked if you wish to [Enter data] or to [Exit SMOOTH]. Type **E** and select the name of the data file to be smoothed. After following the program prompts, you will see the Smoothing Menu which provides a choice of three smoothing methods for the series $\{X_t, t = 1, \ldots, n\}$.

Smooth the data using a symmetric moving average
  The smoothed values are found from

$$\hat{m}_t = \sum_{j=-q}^{q} a(j) X_{t-j}, \quad t = 1, \ldots, n,$$

where $X_t := X_1$ for $t < 1$ and $X_t := X_n$ for $t > n$.

Exponentially smooth the data
  The smoothed values are found from the recursions, $\hat{m}_1 = X_1$ and

$$\hat{m}_t = aX_t + (1 - a)\hat{m}_{t-1}, \quad t = 2, \ldots, n,$$

where a is a specified smoothing constant ($0 \leq a \leq 1$).

Remove high frequency components
  First the discrete Fourier transform,

$$a_j = n^{-1/2} \sum_{t=1}^{n} X_t e^{-it\omega_j}, \quad \omega_j = \frac{2\pi j}{n}, \quad -\frac{n-1}{2} \leq j \leq \frac{n}{2},$$

is computed. Next the coefficients a_j corresponding to frequencies greater in absolute value than $f\pi$ (where f is a parameter between 0 and 1) are set equal to zero. The resulting transform is then inverted to produce the smoothed data,

$$\hat{m}_t = n^{-1/2} \sum_{j:|\omega_j| \leq f\pi} a_j e^{it\omega_j}, \quad j = 1, \ldots, n.$$

3.2   Moving Average Smoothing

If you select the option [Smooth the data using a symmetric moving average] you will be asked to enter the half-length q and the coefficients $a(0), a(1), \ldots, a(q)$ of the required moving average,

$$\hat{m}_t = \sum_{j=-q}^{q} a(j) X_{t-j}, \quad t = 1, \ldots, n,$$

where $a(j) = a(-j)$, $j = 1, \ldots, q$.

The integer q can take any any value greater than or equal to zero and less than $n/2$.

You may enter any real numbers for the coefficients $a(j), j = 0, \ldots, q$. These will automatically be rescaled by the program so that $a(0) + 2a(1) + \cdots + 2a(q) = 1$. (This is achieved by dividing each entered coefficient by the sum $a(0) + 2a(1) + \cdots + 2a(q)$. The program therefore prevents you from entering weights for which this sum is zero.)

Once the parameters $q, a(0), \ldots, a(q)$ have been entered, the program will print on the screen the square root of the average squared deviation of the smoothed values from the original observations, i.e.

$$\text{SQRT(MSE)} = \sqrt{n^{-1} \sum_{j=1}^{n} (\hat{m}_j - X_j)^2}.$$

It will then plot the original data. Typing ↩ will cause the smoothed values to be plotted on the same graph. When plotting has been completed you will be given the option of filing the smoothed values. Finally you will be returned to the menu and offered the four choices listed in Section 3.1.

> EXAMPLE: To smooth the data set STRIKES.DAT using the moving average with weights $a(j) = .2$, $j = -2, -1, 0, 1, 2$, and $a(j) = 0$, $|j| > 2$, use the following sequence of entries (starting from the Smoothing Menu):
>
> $$\mathbf{S} \; \hookleftarrow 2\hookleftarrow 1\hookleftarrow 1\hookleftarrow 1\hookleftarrow \hookleftarrow$$
>
> At this point the screen will display the value
> SQRT(MSE)=1956.142000
>
> Typing ↩ ↩ will then produce the graph displayed in Figure 3.1. The points denoted by squares are the original data and the points joined by a continuous line are the smoothed values.
>
> To file the smoothed values under the file name SMST.DAT, type ↩ **C Y** SMST.DAT ↩ . The smoothed values will then be filed under the name specified and the screen will again display the Smoothing Menu listed above in Section 3.1.

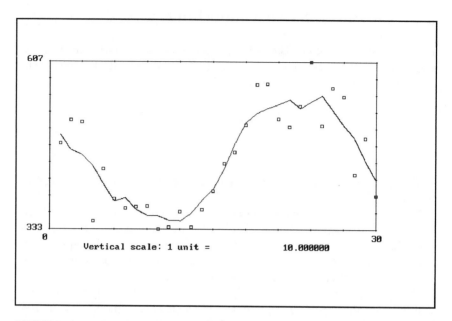

FIGURE 3.1. *The series STRIKES.DAT with smoothed values obtained from a simple moving average of length 5*

3.3 Exponential Smoothing

If you select the option [**Exponentially smooth the data**] you will be asked to enter the parameter a in the smoothing recursions, $\hat{m}_1 = X_1$ and

$$\hat{m}_t = aX_t + (1 - a)\hat{m}_{t-1}, \quad t = 2, \ldots, n.$$

The choice $a = 1$ gives no smoothing ($\hat{m}_t = X_t$, $t = 1, \ldots, n$) while the choice $a = 0$ gives maximum smoothing ($\hat{m}_t = X_1$, $t = 1, \ldots, n$). Enter -1 if you would like the program to select a value for a automatically. This option is particularly useful if you plan to use the smoothed value $\hat{m}_n$ as the predictor of the next observation X_{n+1}. The automatic selection option determines the value of a which minimizes the sum of squares,

$$\sum_{j=2}^{n}(X_j - \hat{m}_{j-1})^2,$$

of the *prediction* errors when each smoothed value $\hat{m}_{j-1}$ is used as the predictor of the *next* observation X_j.

Once the parameter a has been entered (or automatically selected), the program will display the square root of the average squared deviation of the smoothed values from the original observations, i.e.

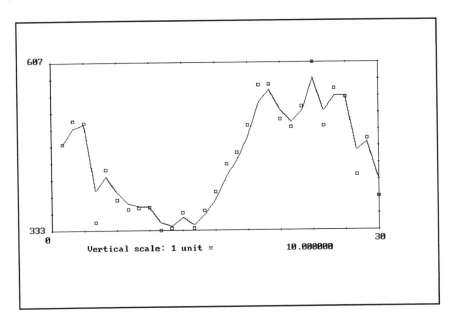

FIGURE 3.2. *The series STRIKES.DAT showing smoothed values obtained by exponential smoothing with parameter a = .68*

$$\text{SQRT(MSE)} = \sqrt{n^{-1} \sum_{j=1}^{n} (\hat{m}_j - X_j)^2}.$$

It will then plot the original data. Typing ↩ will cause the smoothed values to be plotted on the same graph. When plotting has been completed you will be given the option of filing the smoothed values. Finally you will be returned to the menu and offered the four choices listed in Section 3.1.

> EXAMPLE: Continuing with the example in Section 3.2 (again starting from the Smoothing Menu), exponential smoothing of STRIKES.DAT with automatic selection of a can be achieved by typing:
>
> $$\textbf{E} \hookleftarrow -1\hookleftarrow$$
>
> At this point the screen will display the values
>
> | | | |
> |---|---|---|
> | SQRT(MSE) | = | 974.188000 |
> | Parameter a | = | .68 |
>
> Typing ↩ ↩ will then produce the graph displayed in Figure 3.2. The points denoted by squares are the original data and the points joined by a continuous line are the smoothed values.
>
> To file the smoothed values under the file name SMST.DAT, type ↩ **C Y SMST.DAT** ↩ . When filing is completed you will be returned to the Smoothing Menu.

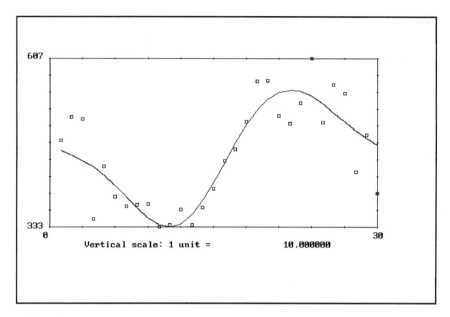

FIGURE 3.3. *The series STRIKES.DAT showing smoothed values obtained by removing Fourier components with frequencies greater than $f\pi$ where $f = .25$*

Exponential smoothing is sometimes used for forecasting. The forecasts of all future data values $X_{n+1}, X_{n+2}, \ldots$, are given by $\hat{m}_n$. For the strikes data, the forecasts of each X_n, $n > 30$ are $\hat{m}_{30} = 4167.38$. Forecasting by exponential smoothing is a simple but crude procedure which uses very little of the information contained in the data. Better forecasts can usually be obtained from the programs *PEST* or *ARAR*.

3.4   Removing High Frequency Components

If you select the option [**Remove high frequency components**] you will be asked to enter a smoothing parameter f between 0 and 1. The smaller the value of f the more the series is smoothed, with maximum smoothing occurring when $f = 0$.

Once the parameter f has been entered, the program will print on the screen the square root of the average squared deviation of the smoothed values from the original observations, i.e.

$$\text{SQRT(MSE)} = \sqrt{n^{-1} \sum_{j=1}^{n} (\hat{m}_j - X_j)^2}.$$

It will then plot the original data. Typing ↵ will cause the smoothed values to be plotted on the same graph. When plotting has been completed you will be given the option of filing the smoothed values. Finally you will be returned to the Smoothing Menu.

> EXAMPLE: Continuing with STRIKES.DAT and starting again from the Smoothing Menu, we can remove the top 75 percent of the frequency components of the data by typing
>
> $$\mathbf{R} \quad .25 \hookleftarrow \quad \hookleftarrow \quad \hookleftarrow$$
>
> The smoothed values are plotted in Figure 3.3. They can be filed exactly as descibed above for moving average and exponential smoothing.

4

SPEC

4.1 Introduction

To run the program *SPEC*, double click on the icon labelled *spec* in the *itsm* window (or in DOS type SPEC↩ from the C:\ITSMW directory). After pressing ↩ to clear the title page, you will see a menu offering the choice of spectral analysis for one or two data sets. For spectral analysis of a univariate series, type **O** and select the name of the data file to be analyzed. Once the data has been read in, a menu will appear which is practically identical to the Spectral Analysis Menu of *PEST* (in the option [**Nonparametric spectral estimation (SPEC)**] of the Main Menu). For instructions on the use of the univariate options available in this menu see Section 2.7.

4.2 Bivariate Spectral Analysis (*BD Section 11.7*)

If you select the bivariate option you will be asked to specify the file names of the two series, $\{X_{t1}, t = 1, \ldots, n\}$ and $\{X_{t2}, t = 1, \ldots, n\}$, to be analyzed. (These are assumed to be stored in separate ASCII files.) Once the series have been read in by the program, you will see the Bivariate Spectral Analysis Menu shown in Figure 4.1.

At this point no weight function has been specified, so the estimated spectral densities of the first and second series, $\hat{f}_{11}$ and $\hat{f}_{22}$, are just the respective periodograms divided by 2π, i.e.

$$\frac{1}{2\pi}I_{11}(\omega_k) = \frac{1}{2\pi}n^{-1}\left|\sum_{t=1}^{n}X_{t1}e^{-it\omega_k}\right|^2,$$
$$\frac{1}{2\pi}I_{22}(\omega_k) = \frac{1}{2\pi}n^{-1}\left|\sum_{t=1}^{n}X_{t2}e^{-it\omega_k}\right|^2,$$

where $\omega_k = 2\pi k/n, k = 0, 1, \ldots, [n/2]$ are the Fourier frequencies in $[0, \pi]$ and $[n/2]$ is the integer part of $n/2$. The cross periodogram is defined as

$$I_{12}(\omega_k) = n^{-1}\left(\sum_{t=1}^{n}X_{t1}e^{-it\omega_k}\right)\overline{\left(\sum_{t=1}^{n}X_{t2}e^{-it\omega_k}\right)}.$$

Without smoothing, the estimated absolute coherency spectrum is

$$|\mathcal{K}_{12}(\omega_k)| = \frac{|I_{12}(\omega_k)|}{I_{11}^{1/2}(\omega_k)I_{22}^{1/2}(\omega_k)} = 1.$$

In order to find a meaningful estimate of the absolute coherency spectrum (and better estimates of the marginal and phase spectra), it is necessary to smooth the periodogram.

```
Number of observations=    149

Mean of series 1 =              .02275168
Variance of series 1 =          .99327340E-01

Mean of series 2 =              .42013410
Variance of series 2 =          .20711380E+01

<Computing the Fourier transform>


MENU : BIVARIATE SPECTRAL ANALYSIS

    ┌──────────────────────────────────────────────────────────┐
    │ Plot estimated f11 (no smoothing; first series)          │
    │ Plot estimated f22 (no smoothing; second series)         │
    │ Plot estimated abs. coherency !K12! (no smoothing)       │
    │ Plot estimated phase spectrum PHI12 (no smoothing)       │
    │ Enter weight function for smoothing                      │
    │ Begin another analysis                                   │
    │ Exit SPEC                                                │
    └──────────────────────────────────────────────────────────┘
```

FIGURE 4.1. *The Bivariate Spectral Analysis Menu*

A weight function $\{W(j), |j| \leq m\}$ for smoothing the periodogram is entered by selecting the option [Enter weight function for smoothing] of the Bivariate Spectral Analysis Menu. After typing **E** ↩ you will be asked to enter a value for m. Type -1 ↩ if a weight function is to be read from a file and 0 ↩ if you wish to return to the Bivariate Spectral Analysis Menu without entering a weight function. If you enter a positive integer value for m, you will be asked to enter the weights $W(0), W(1), \ldots, W(m)$, all of which must be nonnegative. The program ensures that the weight function is symmetric by defining $W(-j) = W(j), j = 1, \ldots, m$ and then rescales the weights so that they add to one. After the weights have been entered, the program returns to the menu which now contains the additional option, [Graph and file the weight function].

4.2.1 ESTIMATING THE SPECTRAL DENSITY OF EACH SERIES

After a weight function $\{W(k)\}$ has been entered, the marginal and cross spectral densities are estimated as

$$
\begin{aligned}
\hat{f}_{11}(\omega_j) &= \frac{1}{2\pi} \sum_{|k| \leq m} W(k) I_{11}(\omega_j + \omega_k), \\
\hat{f}_{22}(\omega_j) &= \frac{1}{2\pi} \sum_{|k| \leq m} W(k) I_{22}(\omega_j + \omega_k), \\
\hat{f}_{12}(\omega_j) &= \frac{1}{2\pi} \sum_{|k| \leq m} W(k) I_{12}(\omega_j + \omega_k).
\end{aligned}
$$

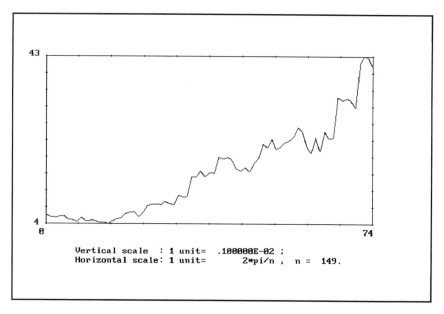

FIGURE 4.2. *Smoothed spectrum estimate for DLEAD.DAT*

The estimates of the marginal densities f_{11} and f_{22} are plotted by selecting the options [Plot estimated f11 for first series] and [Plot estimated f22 for second series] of the Bivariate Spectral Analysis Menu.

> EXAMPLE: Use *PEST* to difference the series LEAD.DAT and SALES.DAT each once at lag 1. File the resulting series as DLEAD.DAT and DSALES.DAT respectively. To conduct a bivariate spectral analysis of DLEAD.DAT and DSALES.DAT, proceed as follows. Run *SPEC* as described above, press ↩ to clear the title page and type **T** to indicate that you wish to analyze two data sets. Select DLEAD.DAT and DSALES.DAT as the first and second series respectively. The Bivariate Spectral Analysis Menu will then appear. To compute smoothed spectral density estimates with weight function $W(0) = W(1) = \cdots = W(6) = \frac{1}{13}$, the first step is to enter the weights by typing **E 6** ↩ 1↩ 1↩ 1↩ 1↩ 1↩ 1↩ (the program automatically rescales the weights so that they add to 1). Plot the weight function by typing **G**. The sequence of entries ↩ **C N** will then return you to the Main Menu. To plot the estimated spectral density of DLEAD.DAT or DSALES.DAT type **P** or **L** respectively (see Figures 4.2 and 4.3). Confidence bounds for the spectral densities of DLEAD.DAT and DSALES.DAT are computed as described in Section 2.7.4.

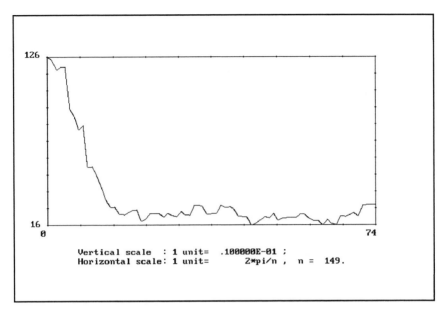

126

16
0   74

Vertical scale : 1 unit= .100000E-01 ;
Horizontal scale: 1 unit=   2*pi/n , n = 149.

FIGURE 4.3. *Smoothed spectrum estimate for DSALES.DAT*

4.2.2   ESTIMATING THE ABSOLUTE COHERENCY SPECTRUM

The absolute coherency spectrum is estimated by

$$|\hat{\mathcal{K}}_{12}(\omega_j)| = \frac{|\hat{f}_{12}(\omega_j)|}{\hat{f}_{11}^{1/2}(\omega_j)\hat{f}_{22}^{1/2}(\omega_j)}$$

where $\hat{f}_{12}(\cdot)$ is the estimate of the cross spectrum given by

$$\hat{f}_{12}(\omega_j) = \frac{1}{2\pi}\sum_{|k|\leq m} W(k)I_{12}(\omega_j + \omega_k).$$

Roughly speaking, the absolute coherency at frequency λ is the absolute value of the correlation between the frequency-λ harmonic components in the two series (see *BD Sections 11.6 and 11.7*). An absolute coherency near 1 indicates a strong linear relationship between the sinusoidal components in the two series.

EXAMPLE: For DLEAD.DAT and DSALES.DAT, select the option [Plot estimated abs. coherency |K12|] of the Bivariate Spectral Analysis Menu to plot the estimated absolute coherency (see Figure 4.4). For this example, the estimated absolute coherency is rather large for all Fourier frequencies. A $100(1-\alpha)\%$

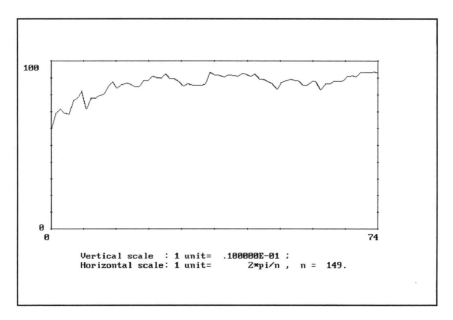

FIGURE 4.4. *Estimated absolute coherency for (DLEAD.DAT,DSALES.DAT)*

confidence interval for $|\mathcal{K}_{12}(\omega_j)|$ is the intersection of $[0, 1]$ with the interval

$$(\tanh[\tanh^{-1}(\hat{\mathcal{K}}_{12}(\omega_j)) - \Phi_{1-\alpha/2}a_n/\sqrt{2}],$$
$$\tanh[\tanh^{-1}(\hat{\mathcal{K}}_{12}(\omega_j)) + \Phi_{1-\alpha/2}a_n/\sqrt{2}]),$$

where $a_n^2 = \sum_{|k|\le m} W^2(k)$ and Φ_α is the α percentile of a standard normal distribution (see *BD equation (11.7.13)*). For this example, $a_n = 1/\sqrt{13}$. The lower limit of the 95% confidence interval for $|\mathcal{K}_{12}(\omega_j)|$ is bounded well away from the 0 which suggests that the absolute coherency is positive for all frequencies.

4.2.3   ESTIMATING THE PHASE SPECTRUM

The phase spectrum, $\phi_{12}(\cdot) \in [-\pi, \pi]$, is defined as $\arg(f_{12}(\lambda))$. The phase spectrum is a measure of the the phase lag of the frequency-λ component of $\{X_{t2}\}$ behind that of $\{X_{t1}\}$. The derivative of $\phi_{12}(\lambda)$ can be interpreted as the time lag by which the frequency-λ component of X_{t2} follows that of X_{t1}. For example if $\phi_{12}(\lambda)$ is piecewise linear with slope d, then X_{t2} lags d time units behind X_{t1}. The phase spectrum is estimated by

$$\hat{\phi}_{12}(\omega_j) = \arg(\hat{f}_{12}(\omega_j))$$

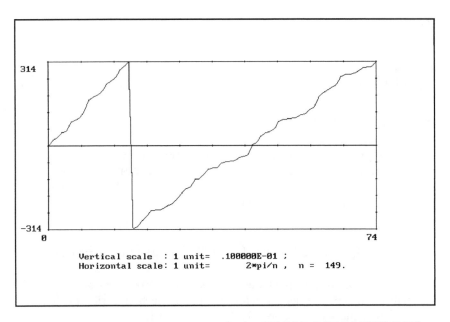

FIGURE 4.5. *Estimated phase spectrum for (DLEAD.DAT,DSALES.DAT)*

EXAMPLE: Continuing with the analysis of the bivariate series (DLEAD.DAT,DSALES.DAT), select the option [Plot estimated phase spectrum PHI12] to plot the estimated phase spec-
trum (see Figure 4.5). The graph of $\hat{\phi}_{12}(\omega_j)$ is roughly piecewise linear with slope 4.1 at the low frequencies and slope 2.7
at higher frequencies. This suggests that DSALES.DAT follows
DLEAD.DAT by approximately 3 time units. A transfer function model with input DLEAD.DAT and output DSALES.DAT
(see Chapter 5 and *BD Section 13.1*) and a bivariate AR model
fitted to the series (DLEAD.DAT,DSALES.DAT) (see Chapter
6 and *BD Section 11.5*) both support this observation.

5

TRANS

5.1 Introduction (*BD Section 13.1*)

To run the program *TRANS*, double click on the icon labelled *trans* in the *itsm* window (or in DOS type TRANS↩ from the C:\ITSMW directory). After pressing ↩ to clear the title page, you will see the Main Menu (Figure 5.1) with five options and two explanatory statements.

5.2 Computing Cross Correlations (*BD Section 11.2*)

If you choose the option [Compute sample cross correlations of two series], you will be asked to select the file names of the first series $\{Y_1(t), t = 1, \ldots, n\}$ and the second series $\{Y_2(t), t = 1, \ldots, n\}$.

You may then calculate the sample cross correlations

$$\hat{\rho}_{Y_1, Y_2}(h) = \hat{\gamma}_{Y_1, Y_2}(h)(\hat{\gamma}_{Y_1, Y_1}(0)\hat{\gamma}_{Y_2, Y_2}(0))^{-1/2}, \ |h| < n,$$

where

$$\hat{\gamma}_{Y_i, Y_j}(h) = \begin{cases} n^{-1}\sum_{t=1}^{n-h}(Y_i(t+h) - \overline{Y}_i)(Y_j(t) - \overline{Y}_j), & h \geq 0, \\ n^{-1}\sum_{t=-h+1}^{n}(Y_i(t+h) - \overline{Y}_i)(Y_j(t) - \overline{Y}_j), & h \leq 0. \end{cases}$$

Alternatively you may apply up to two differencing operators to the two series (the same operators will be applied to both) and compute the sample cross correlations of the differenced series. For example, if you select two differencing operators with lags l_1 and l_2, the program will compute the sample cross correlations of $\{X_1(t)\}$ and $\{X_2(t)\}$, where

$$\begin{aligned} X_1(t) &= (1 - B^{l_1})(1 - B^{l_2})Y_1(t), \quad t = l_1 + l_2 + 1, \ldots, n \\ X_2(t) &= (1 - B^{l_1})(1 - B^{l_2})Y_2(t), \quad t = l_1 + l_2 + 1, \ldots, n, \end{aligned}$$

and B is the backward shift operator (i.e. $B^l Y_i(t) = Y_i(t - l)$).

> EXAMPLE: To compute the sample cross correlations of the two data sets Y_1 =LEAD.DAT and Y_2 =SALES.DAT, select the data files as described above. Then type 0 ↩ to indicate that no differencing is required. Press ↩ and you will see the graph of cross correlations shown in Figure 5.2.

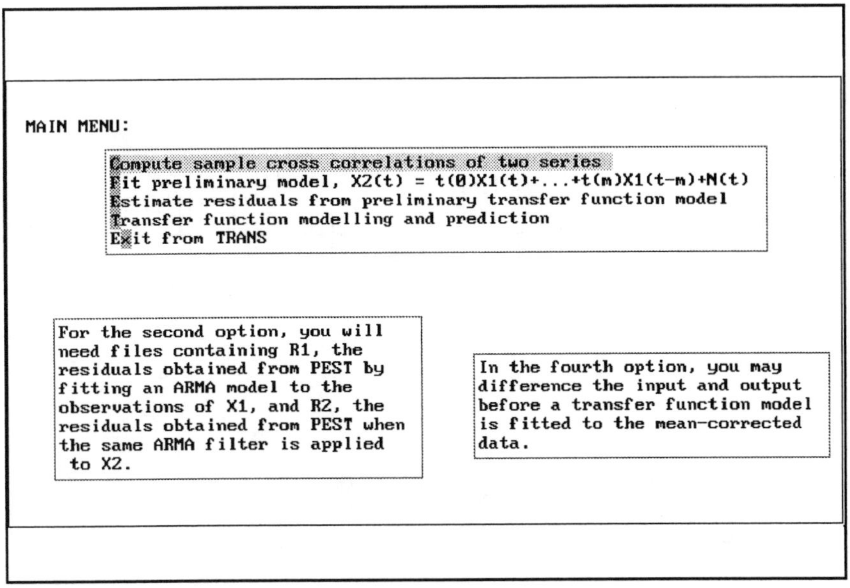

FIGURE 5.1. *The Main Menu of TRANS* .

When you have inspected the graph, press ↩ and you will be asked if you wish to list the sample autocorrelations on the screen. Type **Y** and you will see a listing of $\hat{\rho}_{Y_1,Y_2}(h), h = -30, -29, \ldots, 30$ and be asked whether or not you wish to file the cross correlations. Type **N** and you will then be returned to the Main Menu.

Inspection of the graphs of the two data sets Y_1 =LEAD.DAT and Y_2 =SALES.DAT and their autocorrelations using *PEST* suggests a single differencing at lag 1 to make the series stationary. If X_1 and X_2 denote the series

$$X_i(t) = (1 - B)Y_i(t) = Y_i(t) - Y_i(t-1), \quad i = 1, 2,$$

then the sample autocorrelation function of X_1 and X_2 can be computed using the following entries immediately after reading in the two data files.

1↩ 1↩ ↩ dlead ↩ dsales ↩

At this point the screen will display the graph of cross correlations shown in Figure 5.3. As before, you will be given the options of listing and filing the cross correlations before being returned to the Main Menu.

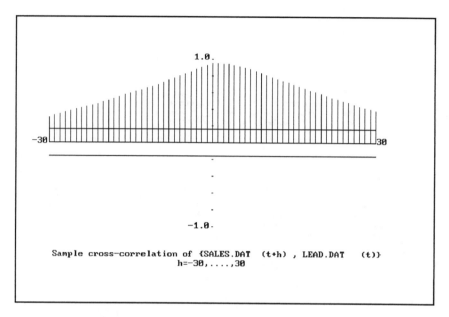

Sample cross-correlation of {SALES.DAT   (t+h) , LEAD.DAT   (t)}
                            h=-30,....,30

FIGURE 5.2. *The cross correlations of LEAD.DAT and SALES.DAT*

5.3   An Overview of Transfer Function Modelling

- Given observations of an "input" series $\{Y_1(t)\}$ and an "output" series $\{Y_2(t)\}$, the steps in setting up a transfer function model relating Y_2 to Y_1 begin with differencing and mean correction to generate transformed input and output series X_1 and X_2 which can be modelled as zero mean stationary processes. Suitable differencing operators (up to two are allowed by *TRANS*) can be found by examination of the series Y_1 and Y_2 using *PEST*. The same differencing operations will be applied to both series.

- An ARMA model is fitted to the transformed input series X_1 using *PEST*, and the residual series R_1 is filed for later use. The same ARMA filter is then applied to X_2 using the option [Likelihood of Model (no optimization)] of the Estimation Menu of *PEST* (to reach the Estimation Menu select [ARMA parameter estimation] from the Main Menu). The residual series R_2 is then filed.

- A preliminary transfer function model relating X_2 to X_1 is found using the option [Fit preliminary model] of *TRANS*. This model has the form,

$$X_2(t) = \sum_{j=0}^{m} t(j)X_1(t-j) + N(t),$$

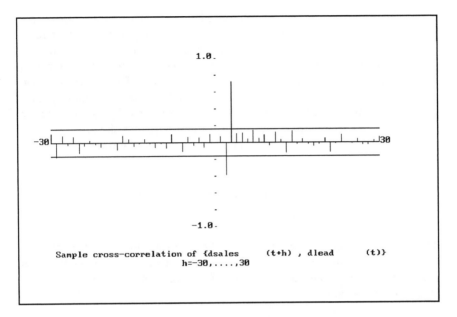

FIGURE 5.3. *The cross correlations of DLEAD and DSALES, obtained by differencing LEAD.DAT and SALES.DAT at lag 1*

where $\{N(t)\}$ is a zero mean stationary noise sequence.

- It is often convenient to replace the transfer function $\sum_{j=0}^{m} t(j)B^j$ by a rational function of B with fewer coefficients. For example, the transfer function,

$$2B + .22B^2 + .018B^3 + .002B^4,$$

could be approximated by the more *parsimonious* transfer function,

$$T(B) = \frac{2B}{1 - .1B}.$$

- Given the series X_1 and X_2 and given any rational transfer function $T(B)$, the option [Estimate residuals from preliminary transfer function model] of *TRANS* calculates values of the noise series $\{N(t)\}$ in the model

$$X_2(t) = T(B)X_1(t) + N(t).$$

- An ARMA model $\phi(B)N(t) = \theta(B)W(t)$ is then fitted to the noise series $\{N(t)\}$. This gives the preliminary transfer function model,

$$X_2(t) = T(B)X_1(t) + \phi^{-1}(B)\theta(B)W(t).$$

- The option [**Transfer function modelling and prediction**] of *TRANS* requires that you enter the preliminary model just determined. It reestimates the coefficients in the preliminary model using least squares. A Kalman filter representation of the model is used to determine minimum mean squared error linear predictors of the output series. Model selection can be made with the AICC statistic, which is computed for each fitted model. Model checking can be carried out by checking the residuals for whiteness and checking the cross correlations of the input residuals and the transfer function residuals.

5.4 Fitting a Preliminary Transfer Function Model

The option [**Fit preliminary model**] of the Main Menu of *TRANS* is concerned with the problem of providing rough estimates of the coefficients $t(0), t(1), \ldots$ in the following model for the relation between two zero-mean stationary time series X_1 and X_2 :

$$X_2(t) = \sum_{j=0}^{\infty} t(j) X_1(t-j) + N(t),$$

where $\{N(t)\}$ is a zero-mean stationary process, uncorrelated with the "input" process X_1. (See *BD Section 13.1* for more details.)

Before using this program it is necessary to have filed the residual series R_1 obtained from *PEST* after fitting an ARMA model to the series X_1. The residual series R_2, obtained by applying the same ARMA filter to the series X_2, is also needed. This is obtained by applying the option [**Likelihood of the Model**] of the Estimation Menu in *PEST* to the data X_2 with the same ARMA model which was fitted to the series X_1. The residuals so obtained constitute the required series R_2.

When [**Fit preliminary model**] is selected from the Main Menu of *TRANS* , you will be asked for the names of the files containing the "input residuals", R_1, and the "output residuals", R_2. You will then be asked for the order of the moving average relating X_2 to X_1. If you specify the order as $m(< 31)$, estimates will be printed on the screen of the coefficients in the relation,

$$X_2(t) = \sum_{j=0}^{m} t(j) X_1(t-j) + N(t).$$

You may wish to print the estimated coefficients $t(j)$ for later use.

To check which of the estimated coefficients are significantly different from zero and to check the appropriateness of the model, we next plot the sample cross correlations of $R_2(t+h)$ and $R_1(t)$ for $h = -30, -29, \ldots, 30$. These correlations $\hat{\rho}(h)$ are directly proportional to the estimates of $t(h)$

(see *BD Section 13.1*). Sample correlations which fall outside the plotted bounds ($\pm 1.96/\sqrt{n}$) are significantly different from zero (with significance level approximately .05). The plotted values $\hat{\rho}(h)$ should therefore lie within the bounds for $h < b$, where b, the smallest non-negative integer such that $|\hat{\rho}(b)| > 1.96/\sqrt{n}$, is our estimate of the delay parameter. Having identified the delay parameter b, the model previously printed on the screen is revised by setting $t(j) = 0$, $j < b$, giving

$$X_2(t) = \sum_{j=b}^{m} t(j) X_1(t - j) + N(t).$$

After inspecting the graph and recording the estimated delay parameter b and coefficients $t(b), \ldots, t(m)$, press any key and you will be returned to the Main Menu.

EXAMPLE: We shall illustrate the use of the option [Fit preliminary model] with reference to the data sets Y_1 =LEAD.DAT and Y_2 =SALES.DAT.

Analysis of these data sets using *PEST* suggests that differencing at lag 1 and subtracting the means from each of the resulting two series gives rise to series X_1 and X_2 which can be well modelled as zero mean stationary series. The values of the two series are

$$X_1(t) = Y_1(t) - Y_1(t-1) - .0228, \quad t = 2, \ldots, 150,$$

$$X_2(t) = Y_2(t) - Y_2(t-1) - .420, \quad t = 2, \ldots, 150,$$

and the ARMA model fitted by *PEST* to X_1 is

$$X_1(t) = Z(t) - .474 Z(t-1), \quad \{Z(t)\} \sim \text{WN}(0, .0779).$$

The residuals R_1 computed from *PEST* have already been filed under the file name LRES.DAT. Likewise the residuals R_2 obtained by applying the filter $(1 - .474B)^{-1}$ to the series X_2 have been filed as SRES.DAT. (To generate the latter from *PEST*, input the data set Y_2, difference at lag 1, subtract the mean, input the MA(1) model $X(t) = Z(t) - .474 Z(t-1)$, and use the option [Likelihood of the Model] of the Estimation Menu to compute and file the residuals.)

To find a preliminary transfer function model relating X_2 to X_1, start from the point where the Main Menu of *TRANS* is displayed upon the screen and type **F**. Select LRES.DAT and SRES.DAT as the "input" and "output" residuals respectively. Press ↩ and type 10↩ . At this point the estimated coefficients

```
Order of MA required, m (<31) : 10
PRELIMINARY TRANSFER COEFFICIENTS:
  t( 0) =              .51802010
  t( 1) =              .66472580
  t( 2) =              .33665350
  t( 3) =             4.86250500
  t( 4) =             3.38969400
  t( 5) =             2.60583300
  t( 6) =             2.00288400
  t( 7) =             2.03665600
  t( 8) =             1.52890200
  t( 9) =             1.32632300
  t(10) =              .78603170

MODEL: X2(j)= t(0)X1(j)+...+t(10)X1(j-10)+ N(t)
           <Press any key to continue>
```

FIGURE 5.4. *The estimated coefficients in the transfer function model relating* X_2 *to* X_1

$t(0), t(1), \ldots, t(10)$, will be displayed on the screen (see Figure 5.4).

On pressing ↩ ↩ , you will then see the sample cross correlations shown in Figure 5.5. It is clear from the graph that the correlations are negligible for lags $h < 3$ and that the estimated delay parameter is $b = 3$. The preliminary model is therefore,

$$X_2(t) = t(3)X_1(t-3) + \cdots + t(10)X_1(t-10) + N(t),$$

where $t(3), \ldots, t(10)$ are as shown in Figure 5.4.

5.5 Calculating Residuals from a Transfer Function Model

The option [Estimate residuals from preliminary transfer function model] of *TRANS* uses observed values of $X_1(t)$ and $X_2(t)$ and a postulated transfer function model,

$$X_2(t) = B^b(w(0) + w(1)B + \cdots + w(r)B^r)(1 - v(1)B - \cdots - v(s)B^s)^{-1}X_1(t)$$

$$+ N(t),$$

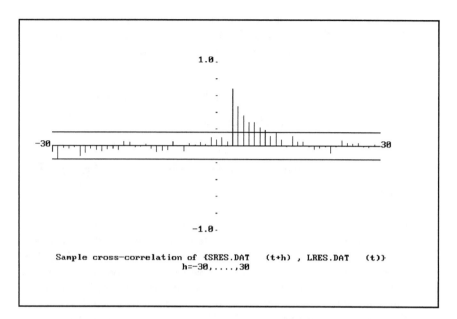

FIGURE 5.5. *The cross correlations of LRES.DAT and SRES.DAT*

to generate estimated values $\hat{N}(t)$, $t > m = \max(r + b, s)$, of $N(t)$. The estimates are evaluated from the preceding equation by setting $N(t) = 0$ for $t \leq m$ and solving for $N(t), t > m$.

EXAMPLE: Continuing with the example of Section 5.4, we observe that the estimated moving average transfer function model relating X_2 to X_1 can be well approximated by a model with fewer coefficients, namely,

$$X_2(t) = 4.86B^3(1 - .7B)^{-1}X_1(t) + N(t).$$

To generate estimated values of the noise, $N(t)$, $3 < t \leq 149$, we first generate the series X_1 and X_2 by appropriate differencing and mean correcting of the input series, LEAD.DAT, and the output series, SALES.DAT. Again start from the Main Menu and type **E**. After selecting LEAD.DAT and SALES.DAT as the input and output series respectively, difference the data at lag 1 by typing 1↩ 1↩ .

Next enter the transfer function $4.86B^3(1 - .7B)^{-1}$ by typing
$$↩ ↩ 3↩ 0↩ 4.86↩ 1↩ .7↩$$

You will then be asked for a file name under which to store $\{\hat{N}(t)\}$. The entries,
$$\text{NOISE.DAT}↩ ↩$$

will cause the 146 noise estimates, $\{\hat{N}(t), t = 4, \ldots, 149\}$, to be stored in the file NOISE.DAT and return you to the Main Menu. Subsequent analysis of this series using *PEST* suggests the model

$$N(t) = (1 - .582B)W(t), \quad \{W(t)\} \sim \mathrm{WN}(0, .0486),$$

for the noise in the transfer function model.

5.6   LS Estimation and Prediction with Transfer Function Models

The option [Transfer function modelling and prediction] requires specification of a previously fitted ARMA model for the input process and a tentatively specified transfer function (including a model for the noise $\{N(t)\}$). It then estimates the parameters in the model by least squares. The exact Gaussian likelihood is computed using a Kalman filter representation of the model, so that different models can be compared on the basis of their AICC statistics. The Kalman filter representation is also used to give exact best linear predictors of the output series using the fitted model. The mean squared errors of the predictors are estimated using a large-sample approximation for the k-step mean squared error.

The first step is to read in the input and output series and to generate the stationary zero mean series X_1 and X_2 by performing up to two differencing operations followed by mean correction.

The next step is to specify the ARMA model fitted to the series X_1 using *PEST* and to specify the delay parameter, b, the orders, r, s, q and p and preliminary estimates of the coefficients in the transfer function model (*BD Section 13.1*),

$$X_2(t) = \frac{B^b(w(0) + w(1)B + \cdots + w(r)B^r)}{1 - v(1)B - \cdots - v(s)B^s} X_1(t)$$

$$+ \frac{1 + \theta(1)B + \cdots + \theta(q)B^q}{1 - \phi(1)B - \cdots - \phi(p)B^p} W(t).$$

When the model has been specified, the Estimation and Prediction Menu will appear as in Figure 5.6.

The option [Least squares estimation] computes least squares estimators of all the parameters in the model and prints out the parameters of the fitted model. Optimization is typically done with gradually decreasing step-sizes, e.g. .1 for the first optimization, then .01 when the first optimization is complete, and .001 or .0001 for the final optimization.

Once the parameters in the model have been estimated, AICC calculation (for comparison of alternative models) and prediction of future values of the

```
ESTIMATION AND PREDICTION MENU :

  Store the current model
  Least squares estimation
  AICC value and prediction
  File residuals and plot cross-correlations
    (access to input residuals filed by PEST
     is needed to plot cross-correlations)
  Try a new model
  Enter a new data set
  Return to main menu
```

FIGURE 5.6. *The Estimation and Prediction Menu*

output series can both be done using the option [**AICC value and prediction**]. Estimated mean squared errors for the predictors are obtained from large-sample approximations to the k-step prediction errors for the fitted model (see *BD Section 13.1*).

To check the goodness of fit of the model, the residuals $\{\hat{W}(t)\}$ should be examined to check that they resemble white noise and that they are uncorrelated with the residuals from the model fitted to the input process. The option [**File residuals and plot cross-correlations**] allows them to be filed for further study and checks the cross correlations with the input residuals, provided the latter have been stored in a file which is currently accessible.

EXAMPLE: Continuing with the example of Section 5.4, we note that the tentative transfer function model we have found relating X_2 to X_1 can now be expressed as,

$$X_2(t) = 4.86B^3(1 - .7B)^{-1}X_1(t) + (1 - .582B)W(t),$$

$$\{W(t)\} \sim \text{WN}(0, .0486),$$

where

$$X_1(t) = (1 - .474B)Z(t), \quad \{Z(t)\} \sim \text{WN}(0, .0779).$$

Starting from the screen display of the Main Menu, we first select the option [**Transfer function modelling and prediction**] and

```
CURRENT MODEL PARAMETERS ARE:
   b    =    3
   w(0)  =     4.91000000
   v(1)  =      .70000000
   th(1) =     -.43200000
INPUT AND OUTPUT WN VARIANCES
.77900000E-01  .59163400E-01

INPUT MA COEFFS
 -4.740000E-01
   <Press any key to continue>
```

FIGURE 5.7. *The fitted model after using least squares with step-size .1*

generate the series X_1 and X_2 by appropriate differencing and mean correcting of the input series, LEAD.DAT, and the output series, SALES.DAT.

After the data has been successfully entered and differenced, the model previously fitted to X_1 and the orders and coefficients of the tentative transfer function model found in Section 5.4 are now entered as follows :

$$\hookleftarrow \hookleftarrow 0\hookleftarrow 1\hookleftarrow -.474\hookleftarrow .0779\hookleftarrow 3\hookleftarrow$$
$$0\hookleftarrow 4.86\hookleftarrow 1\hookleftarrow .7\hookleftarrow 1\hookleftarrow -.582\hookleftarrow 0\hookleftarrow \hookleftarrow$$

The specified model will then be displayed on the screen. Press any key to see the Estimation and Prediction Menu shown in Figure 5.6.

To obtain least squares estimates of the transfer function coefficients, select the option [**Least squares estimation**] with step-size .1 by typing

$$\mathbf{L} \ .1\hookleftarrow$$

There will be a short delay while optimization is performed. The screen will then display the new fitted coefficients and white noise variance, as shown in Figure 5.7.

To refine the estimates, optimize again with step-size .01 by typing $\hookleftarrow \mathbf{L} \ .01\hookleftarrow$ and again with step-size .001 by typing

```
CURRENT MODEL PARAMETERS ARE:
    b     =     3

    w(0)  =     4.71899700

    v(1)  =      .72449990

    th(1) =     -.58249980
INPUT AND OUTPUT WN VARIANCES
 .77900000E-01  .48644480E-01

INPUT MA COEFFS
 -4.740000E-01
    <Press any key to continue>
```

FIGURE 5.8. *The fitted model after two further optimizations with step-sizes .01 and .001*

$\hookleftarrow$ **L** .001$\hookleftarrow$. The resulting fitted model is shown in Figure 5.8.

Future values of the original output series SALES.DAT may be predicted with the fitted model by selecting the option [**AICC value and prediction**] of the Estimation and Prediction Menu. To predict the next 10 values of SALES.DAT, type **A** 10$\hookleftarrow$. (After typing **A** in ITSM41, the following warning will be displayed on your screen:

```
Some mathematics coprocessors will have underflow
problems in this option.  If this occurs you will
need to exit from TRANS,switch off the coprocessor
and rerun this option.   The DOS command required
to switch off the coprocessor is
   SET no87=COPROCESSOR OFF
To switch it on again use the command
   SET no87=

If you have not already filed the current model, it
may save time to do so now.

Do you wish to file the model (y/n)?
```

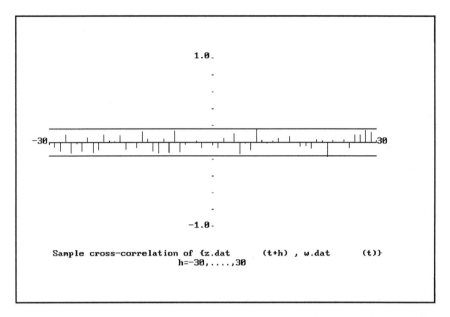

FIGURE 5.9. *The sample cross correlations of the residual series W.DAT and Z.DAT*

If this warning is applicable to your mathematics coprocessor, you must turn if off as described in the above message. Assuming that this is not necessary, continue by typing **N** 10↩). After a short delay you will see the message

```
AICC value = .277041E+02
```

Typing ↩ gives ten predicted values of SALES.DAT, together with the estimated root mean squared errors. The mean squared errors are computed from the large sample approximations described in *BD Section 13.1*. Type ↩ **Y** ↩ and the original output series will be plotted on the screen. Then press any key and the predictors will also be plotted on the same graph. Type ↩ **C N** ↩ to return to the Estimation and Prediction Menu.

To check the goodness of fit of the model, the option [**File residuals and plot cross-correlations**] of this menu allows you to file the estimated residuals $\hat{W}(t)$ from the transfer function model and to check for zero cross-correlations with the input residuals R_1. To do this type

F W.DAT↩ **Y** LRES.DAT↩ Z.DAT↩ ↩

At this point the estimated residuals, $\hat{W}(t), 3 < t \leq 149$, will have been stored under the filename W.DAT and the corresponding 146 values of $R_1(t)$ under the filename Z.DAT. You will see on the screen the sample cross-correlations of these two sets of residuals. For a good fit, approximately 95% of the plotted values should lie within the plotted bounds. Inspection of the graph shown in Figure 5.9 indicates that the fitted model is satisfactory from the point of view of residual cross correlations. (The sample autocorrelations of the residuals filed in W.DAT and Z.DAT are also found, using *PEST*, to be consistent with those of white noise sequences.)

After inspecting the graph of sample cross correlations, type ↩ ↩ and you will be returned to the Estimation and Prediction Menu.

The option [**Try a new model**] allows you to input a different preliminary model, for which the preceding analysis can be repeated. Different models can be compared on the basis of their AICC statistics.

The option [**Enter a new data set**] allows you to input a new data set.

The last option returns you to the Main Menu.

6

ARVEC

6.1 Introduction

The program *ARVEC* fits a multivariate autoregression of any specified order $p < 21$ to a multivariate time series $\{\mathbf{Y}_t = (Y_{t1}, \ldots, Y_{tm})', t = 1, \ldots, n\}$. To run the program, double click on the icon *arvec* in the *itsmw* window (or type `ARVEC` $\hookleftarrow$ from the DOS prompt) and you will see a title page followed by a brief introductory statement describing the program. After reading this statement, follow the program prompts, selecting the option [Enter data] by typing the highlighted letter **E**. You will then be asked to enter the dimension $m \leq 6$ ($m \leq 11$ for *ITSM50*) of $\mathbf{Y}_t$ and to select the file containing the observations $\{\mathbf{Y}_t, t = 1, \ldots, n\}$. For example, to model the bivariate data set LS2.DAT you would enter the dimension $m = 2$ and then select the file LS2.DAT from the list of data files. The data must be stored as an ASCII file such that row t contains the m components, $\mathbf{Y}_t = (Y_{t1}, \ldots, Y_{tm})'$, each separated by at least one blank space. (The sample size n can be at most 700 for *ITSM41* and 10000 for *ITSM50*.) The value of n will then be printed on the screen and you will be given the option of plotting the component series.

Examination of the graphs of the component series and their autocorrelations (which can be checked using *PEST*) indicates whether differencing transformations should be applied to the series $\{\mathbf{Y}_t\}$ before attempting to fit an autoregressive model. After inspecting the graphs you will therefore be asked if you wish to difference the data and, if so, to enter the number of differencing transformations required (0, 1 or 2) and the corresponding lags. If, for example, you request two differencing operations with LAG(1)=1 and LAG(2)=12, then the series $\{\mathbf{Y}_t\}$ will be transformed to the differenced series, $(1-B)(1-B^{12})\mathbf{Y}_t = \mathbf{Y}_t - \mathbf{Y}_{t-1} - \mathbf{Y}_{t-12} + \mathbf{Y}_{t-13}$. The resulting differenced data is then automatically mean-corrected to generate the series $\{\mathbf{X}_t\}$. To fit a multivariate autoregression to the series $\{\mathbf{X}_t\}$ you can either specify the order of the autoregression to be fitted or select the automatic minimum AICC option. The estimation algorithm is given in the following section.

6.1.1   MULTIVARIATE AUTOREGRESSION (*BD Sections 11.3–11.5*)

An m-variate time series $\{\mathbf{X}_t\}$ is said to be a (causal) *multivariate* AR(p) process if it satisfies the recursions

$$\mathbf{X}_t = \Phi_{p1}\mathbf{X}_{t-1} + \cdots + \Phi_{pp}\mathbf{X}_{t-p} + \mathbf{Z}_t, \qquad \{\mathbf{Z}_t\} \sim \mathrm{WN}(0, V_p),$$

where $\Phi_{p1}, \ldots, \hat{\Phi}_{pp}$ are $m \times m$ coefficient matrices, V_p is the error covariance matrix, and $\det(I - z\Phi_{p1} - \cdots - z^p\Phi_{pp}) \neq 0$ for all $|z| \leq 1$. (The first subscript p of Φ_{pj} represents the order of the autoregression.) The coefficient matrices and the error covariance matrix satisfy the multivariate Yule-Walker equations,

$$\sum_{j=1}^p \Phi_{pj}\Gamma(i - j) = \Gamma(i), \qquad i = 1, \ldots, p,$$

$$\Gamma(0) - \sum_{j=1}^p \Phi_{pj}\Gamma(-j) = V_p.$$

Given observations $\mathbf{x}_1, \ldots, \mathbf{x}_n$ of a zero-mean stationary m-variate time series, *ARVEC* determines (for a specified value of p) the AR(p) model defined by

$$\mathbf{X}_t = \hat{\Phi}_{p1}\mathbf{X}_{t-1} + \cdots + \hat{\Phi}_{pp}\mathbf{X}_{t-p} + \mathbf{Z}_t, \qquad \{\mathbf{Z}_t\} \sim \mathrm{WN}(0, \hat{V}_p),$$

where $\hat{\Phi}_{p1}, \ldots, \hat{\Phi}_{pp}$ and $\hat{V}_p$ satisfy the Yule-Walker equations above with $\Gamma(h)$ replaced by the sample covariance matrix $\hat{\Gamma}(h), h = 0, 1, \ldots, p$. The coefficient estimates are computed using Whittle's multivariate version of the Durbin-Levinson algorithm (*BD Section 11.4*).

> EXAMPLE: Let us now use *ARVEC* to model and forecast the bi-variate leading indicator-sales data, $\{(Y_{t1}, Y_{t2})', t = 1, \ldots, 150\}$ contained in the ASCII file LS2.DAT. Double click on the *arvec* icon in the *itsmw* window and you will see the *arvec* title page. Type $\hookleftarrow$ and you will see the introductory description of the program. Then type
>
> $$\hookleftarrow \mathbf{E}\ 2\hookleftarrow,$$
>
> and select LS2.DAT from the list of data files by moving the highlight bar over the entry LS2.DAT and pressing $\hookleftarrow$. (In *ITSM50*, you must first move the highlight bar over <DATA> and press $\hookleftarrow$ to view the data files.) After the data has been read into *ARVEC*, a menu will appear giving you the option of plotting either of the component series. After inspecting the graphs of the component series, type **C** to continue and you will then be asked the question,
>
> Do you wish to difference the data?

The graphs suggest that both series should be differenced at lag 1 to generate data which are more compatible with realizations from a stationary process. To apply the differencing operator $1 - B$ to $\{Y_t\}$, type **Y** **1** $\hookleftarrow$ **1** $\hookleftarrow$. The program then computes the mean-corrected series,

$$\left[\begin{array}{c} X_{t1} \\ X_{t2} \end{array} \right] = \left[\begin{array}{c} Y_{t1} - Y_{t-1,1} \\ Y_{t2} - Y_{t-1,2} \end{array} \right] - \left[\begin{array}{c} .02275 \\ .42013 \end{array} \right]$$

for $t = 2, \ldots, 150$. At this stage, you have the opportunity to plot the differenced and mean-corrected series to check for any obvious deviations from stationarity (after which you can also change the differencing operations if necessary). In this example, type **N** in response to the question

Try new differencing operations ?

since the single differencing at lag 1 appears to be satisfactory. You will then be asked to choose between the options [**F**ind minimum AICC model], [**S**pecify order for fitted model] and [**E**xit from ARVEC]. If you choose the second option by typing **S** you will then be asked to specify the order $p(< 21)$ of the multivariate AR process to be fitted to $\{X_t\}$. Try fitting an AR(2) model by typing **2**$\hookleftarrow$. The screen will then display the estimated coefficient matrices $\hat{\Phi}_{21}, \hat{\Phi}_{22}$ in the following format:

```
PHI( 1)
-.5096E+00      .2645E-01
-.7227E+00      .2809E+00

PHI( 2)
-.1511E+00     -.1033E-01
-.2148E+01      .2045E+00

<Press any key to continue>
```

Type $\hookleftarrow$ and you will see the estimated white noise covariance matrix and the AICC statistic (for order selection). To return to the point at which a new value of p may be entered, type $\hookleftarrow$ **N** **N** **Y**. The choice $p = 0$ will result in a white noise fit to the data. Selection of the option [**F**ind minimum AICC model] will cause the program to find the model with the smallest AICC value (see Section 6.2 below).

6.2   Model Selection with the AICC Criterion (*BD Section 11.5*)

The Akaike information criterion (AIC) is a commonly used criterion for choosing the order of a model. This criterion prevents overfitting of a model by effectively assigning a cost to the introduction of each additional parameter. For an m-variate AR(p) process the AICC statistic (a bias-corrected modification of the AIC) computed by the program is

$$\text{AICC} = -2\ln L(\hat{\Phi}_{p1}, \ldots, \hat{\Phi}_{pp}, \hat{V}_p) + 2(pm^2 + 1)nm/(nm - pm^2 - 2),$$

where L is the Gaussian likelihood of the model based on the n observations, and $\hat{\Phi}_{p1}, \ldots, \hat{\Phi}_{pp}, \hat{V}_p$ are the Yule-Walker estimates described in Section 6.1. The order p of the model is chosen to minimize the AICC statistic.

> EXAMPLE: For the differenced and mean-corrected LS2.DAT series, the optimal order is found by selecting the option [**Find minimum AICC model**] instead of the option [**Specify order for fitted model**] chosen previously. For this example the optimal order is 5 with AICC=109.49. The fact that the upper right component of each of the coefficient estimates is near 0 suggests that $\{X_{t1}\}$ could be modelled independently of $\{X_{t2}\}$. Also note that the first large component in the bottom left corner of the coefficient matrices occurs at lag 3. This suggests that $\{X_{t2}\}$ lags 3 time units behind $\{X_{t1}\}$ (see *BD Example 11.5.1*).

6.3   Forecasting with the Fitted Model (*BD Sections 11.4, 11.5*)

After the fitted model is displayed, the entries ↵ **Y** 10↵ will produce forecasts of the next 10 values of $\mathbf{X}_t$. To examine the forecasts and the corresponding standard errors (**SQRT(MSE)**) of a given component of the series $\{\mathbf{X}_t\}$ or $\{\mathbf{Y}_t\}$ proceed as in the following example.

> EXAMPLE: From the point at which the AICC value of the optimal AR(5) model is displayed on the screen, the forecasts of sales for the next 10 time periods are found by typing ↵ **Y** 10 **C** 2 (see Figure 6.1). The forecast of sales at time 153 is 263.4 with a standard error of .5640. Approximate 95% prediction bounds based on the fitted AR(5) model and assuming that the noise is Gaussian are therefore,

$$263.4 \pm (1.96)(.564).$$

```
FORECASTS :
     TIME        ORIG. Y2          SQRT(MSE)
     151        .2629E+03         .3084E+00
     152        .2641E+03         .4254E+00
     153        .2634E+03         .5640E+00
     154        .2636E+03         .1460E+01
     155        .2639E+03         .2187E+01
     156        .2642E+03         .2874E+01
     157        .2644E+03         .3539E+01
     158        .2647E+03         .4236E+01
     159        .2650E+03         .4900E+01
     160        .2654E+03         .5548E+01
<Press any key to continue>
```

FIGURE 6.1. *Forecasts of the next 10 sales values*

To plot the sales data and the 10 predictors, type ↩ **Y** ↩
↩ To get the forecasts of the leading indicator series 10 steps
ahead, press any key and type **C 1**.

After escaping from the forecasting part of *ARVEC*, you will be given
the option to file the one-step prediction errors for $\{\mathbf{X}_t\}$,

$$\mathbf{X}_t - \hat{\mathbf{\Phi}}_{p1}\mathbf{X}_{t-1} - \cdots - \hat{\mathbf{\Phi}}_{pp}\mathbf{X}_{t-p}, \qquad t = p+1, \ldots, n$$

and to fit a different model (i.e. one with a different value of p) to the series
$\{\mathbf{X}_t\}$.

7

BURG

7.1 Introduction

Like *ARVEC*, the program *BURG* fits a multivariate autoregression (of order $p < 21$) to a multivariate time series $\{\mathbf{Y}_t = (Y_{t1}, \ldots, Y_{tm})', t = 1, \ldots, n\}$. To run the program, double click on the icon *burg* in the *itsmw* window (or type BURG $\hookleftarrow$ from the DOS prompt) and you will see a title page followed by a brief introductory statement describing the program. After reading this statement, follow the program prompts, selecting the option [Enter data] by typing the highlighted letter **E**. You will then be asked to enter the dimension $m \leq 6$ ($m \leq 11$ for *ITSM50*) of $\mathbf{Y}_t$ and to select the file containing the observations $\{\mathbf{Y}_t, t = 1, \ldots, n\}$. For example, to model the bivariate data set LS2.DAT you would enter the dimension $m = 2$ and then select the file LS2.DAT from the list of data files. The data must be stored as an ASCII file such that row t contains the m components, $\mathbf{Y}_t = (Y_{t1}, \ldots, Y_{tm})'$, each separated by at least one blank space. (The sample size n can be at most 700 for *ITSM41* and 10000 for *ITSM50*.) The value of n will then be printed on the screen and you will be given the option of plotting the component series.

Examination of the graphs of the component series and their autocorrelations (which can be checked using *PEST*) indicates whether differencing transformations should be applied to the series $\{\mathbf{Y}_t\}$ before attempting to fit an autoregressive model. After inspecting the graphs you will therefore be asked if you wish to difference the data and, if so, to enter the number of differencing transformations required (0, 1 or 2) and the corresponding lags. If, for example, you request two differencing operations with LAG(1)=1 and LAG(2)=12, then the series $\{\mathbf{Y}_t\}$ will be transformed to the differenced series, $(1-B)(1-B^{12})\mathbf{Y}_t = \mathbf{Y}_t - \mathbf{Y}_{t-1} - \mathbf{Y}_{t-12} + \mathbf{Y}_{t-13}$. The resulting differenced data is then automatically mean-corrected to generate the series $\{\mathbf{X}_t\}$. To fit a multivariate autoregression to the series $\{\mathbf{X}_t\}$ you can either specify the order of the autoregression to be fitted or select the automatic minimum AICC option.

The only difference between *ARVEC* and *BURG* lies in the fitting algorithm, which for the latter is the multivariate version of the Burg algorithm due to R.H. Jones. Details are given in the book *Applied Time Series Analysis*, ed. D. Findley, Academic Press, 1978. We shall therefore confine ourselves here to a reanalysis, using *BURG*, of the example given in Chapter 6.

EXAMPLE: We shall use *BURG* to fit a multivariate AR(p) model to the differenced leading indicator-sales series as was done in Chapter 6 using *ARVEC* . Double click on the *burg* icon in the *itsmw* window and you will see the *burg* title page. Type ↵ and you will see the introductory description of the program. After typing

$$↵ \textbf{E } 2↵,$$

select LS2.DAT from the list of data files by moving the highlight bar over the entry LS2.DAT and pressing ↵ . (To view the data files in *ITSM50*, you must first move the highlight bar over <DATA> and press ↵ .) Once the data has been read into *BURG*, a menu will appear giving you the option of plotting either of the component series. After inspecting the graphs of the component series, type **C** to continue and you will then be asked the question,

`Do you wish to difference the data?`

Inspection of the graphs of the component series suggests that both series should be differenced at lag 1 to generate data which are more compatible with realizations from a stationary process. To apply the differencing operator $1-B$ to $\{\mathbf{Y}_t\}$, type **Y** 1 ↵ 1 ↵ . The program then computes the mean-corrected series,

$$\begin{bmatrix} X_{t1} \\ X_{t2} \end{bmatrix} = \begin{bmatrix} Y_{t1} - Y_{t-1,1} \\ Y_{t2} - Y_{t-1,2} \end{bmatrix} - \begin{bmatrix} .02275 \\ .42013 \end{bmatrix}$$

for $t = 2, \ldots, 150$. At this stage, you have the opportunity to plot the differenced and mean-corrected series to check for any obvious deviations from stationarity (after which you can also change the differencing operations if necessary). In this example, type **N** in response to the question

`Try new differencing operations ?`

since the single differencing at lag 1 appears to be satisfactory. You will then be asked to choose between the options [**Find minimum AICC model**], [**Specify order for fitted model**] and [**Exit from ARVEC**]. If you choose the second option by typing **S** you will be asked to specify the order $p(< 21)$ of the multivariate AR process to be fitted to $\{\mathbf{X}_t\}$. Try fitting an AR(2) model by typing 2 ↵ . The screen will then display the estimated coefficient matrices $\hat{\Phi}_{21}, \hat{\Phi}_{22}$ in the following format:

```
PHI( 1)
 -.5129E+00      .2662E-01
 -.7341E+00      .2816E+00
```

```
PHI( 2)
-.1526E+00    -.1055E-01
-.2168E+01     .2054E+00
```

```
<Press any key to continue>
```

Type ↩ and you will see the estimated white noise covariance matrix and the AICC statistic (for order selection). To return to the point at which a new value of p may be entered, type ↩ **N N Y**. The choice $p = 0$ will result in a white noise fit to the data. Automatic order selection is obtained by selecting the option [**Find minimum AICC model**] instead of the option [**Specify order for fitted model**] chosen previously. For this example the minimum AICC *BURG* model has order 8 with AICC=56.32.

The first large component in the bottom left corner of the coefficient matrices occurs again at lag 3 suggesting that $\{X_{t2}\}$ lags 3 time units behind $\{X_{t1}\}$ (see *BD Example 11.5.1*).

From the point at which the AICC value of the AR(8) model is displayed on the screen, the forecasts of sales for the next 10 time periods are found by typing ↩ **Y** 10 **C** 2 (see Figure 7.1). The forecast of sales at time 153 is 263.5 with a standard error of .2566. Approximate 95% prediction bounds based on the fitted AR(5) model and assuming that the noise is Gaussian are therefore,

$$263.5 \pm (1.96)(.257).$$

The predicted value is very close to the value obtained from *ARVEC* but the standard error (assuming the validity of the *BURG* model) is smaller than for the *ARVEC* model. To plot the sales data and the 10 predictors, type ↩ **Y** ↩ ↩ . To get the forecasts of the leading indicator series 10 steps ahead, press any key and type **C** 1.

After escaping from the forecasting part of *BURG*, you will be given the option to file the one-step prediction errors for $\{X_t\}$,

$$\mathbf{X}_t - \hat{\mathbf{\Phi}}_{p1}\mathbf{X}_{t-1} - \cdots - \hat{\mathbf{\Phi}}_{pp}\mathbf{X}_{t-p}, \qquad t = p+1, \ldots, n,$$

and to fit a different model (i.e. one with a different value of p) to the series $\{\mathbf{X}_t\}$. The one-step prediction errors should resemble a multivariate white noise sequence if the fitted model is appropriate. Goodness of fit can therefore be tested by checking if the minimum AICC model for the prediction errors has order $p = 0$. This test can be carried out for our current example as follows.

```
FORECASTS :
    TIME        ORIG. Y2          SQRT(MSE)
     151       .2629E+03         .2058E+00
     152       .2643E+03         .2308E+00
     153       .2635E+03         .2566E+00
     154       .2641E+03         .1295E+01
     155       .2643E+03         .2035E+01
     156       .2649E+03         .2741E+01
     157       .2653E+03         .3431E+01
     158       .2658E+03         .4148E+01
     159       .2660E+03         .4848E+01
     160       .2666E+03         .5604E+01
<Press any key to continue>
```

FIGURE 7.1. *Forecasts of the next 10 sales values*

EXAMPLE: Continuing from the displayed list of forecasts of the leading indicator series, type ↩ **N C Y res.dat** ↩ . These commands will store the one-step prediction errors (or residuals) in a data file called RES.DAT. Then type **N E 2** ↩ and read in the new data file RES.DAT using the highlight bar. Then type ↩ **C N** ↩ **C N F**. At this point you will see that the fitted minimum AICC model for RES.DAT has order $p = 0$, the only estimated parameter being the white noise covariance matrix. This lends support to the goodness of fit of the minimum AICC AR(8) model fitted by *BURG* to the series $\{X_t\}$.

8

ARAR

8.1 Introduction

To run the program *ARAR*, double click on the *arar* icon in the *itsmw* window (or type **ARAR**↩ from the DOS prompt) and press ↩ . You will then see a brief introductory statement. The program is an adaptation of the ARARMA forecasting scheme of Newton and Parzen (see *The Accuracy of Major Forecasting Procedures*, ed. Makridakis et al., John Wiley, 1984, pp.267 - 287). The latter was found to perform extremely well in the forecasting competition of Makridakis, the results of which are described in the book. The ARARMA scheme has a further advantage over most standard forecasting techniques in being more readily automated.

On typing ↩ you will be given the options [**Enter a new data set**] and [**Exit from ARAR**]. Choose the first of these by typing **E** and you will see the list of data files from which you can select by moving the highlight bar over the desired filename with the arrow keys and pressing ↩ . (To view the data files in *ITSM50*, you must first move the highlight bar over <DATA> and press ↩ .) Once you have selected a data set and pressed ↩ you will see the Main Menu shown in Figure 8.1.

8.1.1 MEMORY SHORTENING

Given a data set $\{Y_t, t = 1, 2, \ldots, n\}$, the first step is to decide whether or not the process is "long-memory", and if so to apply a memory-shortening transformation before attempting to fit an autoregressive model. The differencing operations permitted by *PEST* are examples of memory-shortening transformations, however the ones allowed by *ARAR* are more general. There are two types allowed :

$$\tilde{Y}_t = Y_t - \hat{\phi}(\hat{\tau})Y_{t-\hat{\tau}} \tag{1}$$

and

$$\tilde{Y}_t = Y_t - \hat{\phi}_1 Y_{t-1} - \hat{\phi}_2 Y_{t-2}. \tag{2}$$

With the aid of the five-step algorithm described below, we shall classify $\{Y_t\}$ and take one of the following three courses of action.

- **L.** Declare $\{Y_t\}$ to be long-memory and form $\{\tilde{Y}_t\}$ using (1).

- **M.** Declare $\{Y_t\}$ to be moderately long-memory and form $\{\tilde{Y}_t\}$ using (2).

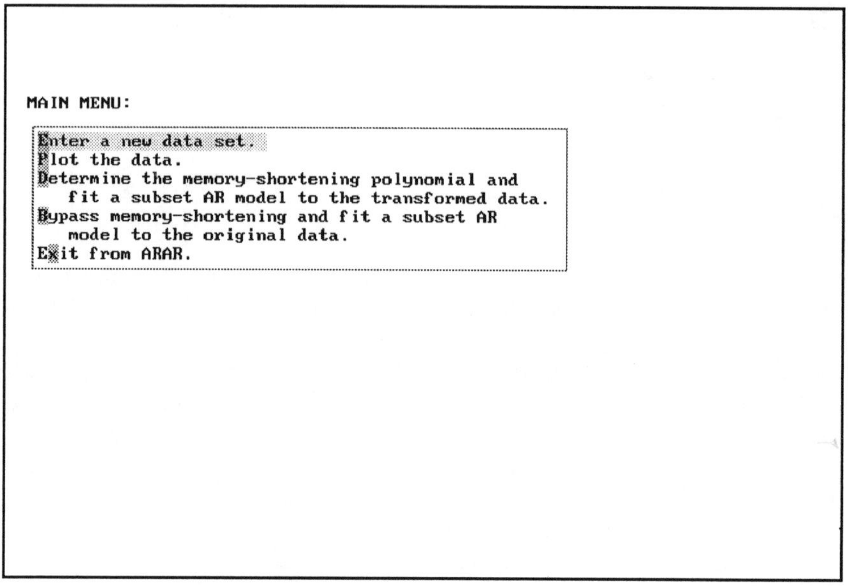

```
MAIN MENU:

  Enter a new data set.
  Plot the data.
  Determine the memory-shortening polynomial and
     fit a subset AR model to the transformed data.
  Bypass memory-shortening and fit a subset AR
     model to the original data.
  Exit from ARAR.
```

FIGURE 8.1. *The main menu of ARAR*

- **S.** Declare $\{Y_t\}$ to be short-memory.

If the alternatives L or M are chosen then the transformed series $\{\tilde{Y}_t\}$ is again checked. If it is found to be long-memory or moderately long-memory, then a further transformation is performed. The process continues until the transformed series is classified as short-memory. The program *ARAR* allows at most three memory-shortening transformations. It is very rare to require more than two. The algorithm for deciding between L, M and S can be described as follows:

1. For each $\tau = 1, 2, \ldots, 15$, we find the value $\hat{\phi}(\tau)$ of ϕ which minimizes

$$\text{Err}(\phi, \tau) = \frac{\sum_{t=\tau+1}^{n} [Y_t - \phi Y_{t-\tau}]^2}{\sum_{t=\tau+1}^{n} Y_t^2}.$$

We then define

$$\text{Err}(\tau) = \frac{\sum_{t=\tau+1}^{n} [Y_t - \hat{\phi}(\tau) Y_{t-\tau}]^2}{\sum_{t=\tau+1}^{n} Y_t^2},$$

and choose the lag $\hat{\tau}$ to be the value of τ which minimizes $\text{Err}(\tau)$.

2. If $\text{Err}(\hat{\tau}) \leq 8/n$, go to L.

3. If $\hat{\phi}(\hat{\tau}) \geq .93$ and $\hat{\tau} > 2$, go to L.

4. If $\hat{\phi}(\hat{\tau}) \geq .93$ and $\hat{\tau} = 1$ or 2, determine the values $\hat{\phi}_1$ and $\hat{\phi}_2$ of ϕ_1 and ϕ_2 which minimize

$$\sum_{t=3}^{n}[Y_t - \phi_1 Y_{t-1} - \phi_2 Y_{t-2}]^2.$$

Go to M.

5. If $\hat{\phi}(\hat{\tau}) < .93$, go to S.

8.1.2   FITTING A SUBSET AUTOREGRESSION

Let $\{S_t, t = 1,\ldots,T\}$ denote the memory-shortened series derived from $\{Y_t\}$ by the algorithm of the previous section and let $\overline{S}$ denote the sample mean of $S_1,\ldots,S_T$.

The next step in the modelling procedure is to fit an autoregressive process to the mean-corrected series,

$$X_t = S_t - \overline{S}, \quad t = 1,\ldots,T.$$

The fitted model has the form

$$X_t = \phi_1 X_{t-1} + \phi_{l_1} X_{t-l_1} + \phi_{l_2} X_{t-l_2} + \phi_{l_3} X_{t-l_3}$$

$$+ Z_t,$$

where $\{Z_t\} \sim \text{WN}(0, \sigma^2)$, and, for given lags, l_1, l_2, and l_3, the coefficients ϕ_j and the white noise variance σ^2 are found from the Yule-Walker equations,

$$\begin{bmatrix} 1 & \hat{\rho}(l_1-1) & \hat{\rho}(l_2-1) & \hat{\rho}(l_3-1) \\ \hat{\rho}(l_1-1) & 1 & \hat{\rho}(l_2-l_1) & \hat{\rho}(l_3-l_1) \\ \hat{\rho}(l_2-1) & \hat{\rho}(l_2-l_1) & 1 & \hat{\rho}(l_3-l_2) \\ \hat{\rho}(l_3-1) & \hat{\rho}(l_3-l_1) & \hat{\rho}(l_3-l_2) & 1 \end{bmatrix} \begin{bmatrix} \phi_1 \\ \phi_{l_1} \\ \phi_{l_2} \\ \phi_{l_3} \end{bmatrix}$$

$$= \begin{bmatrix} \hat{\rho}(1) \\ \hat{\rho}(l_1) \\ \hat{\rho}(l_2) \\ \hat{\rho}(l_3) \end{bmatrix},$$

and

$$\sigma^2 = \hat{\gamma}(0)[1 - \phi_1\hat{\rho}(1) - \phi_{l_1}\hat{\rho}(l_1) - \phi_{l_2}\hat{\rho}(l_2) - \phi_{l_3}\hat{\rho}(l_3)],$$

where $\hat{\gamma}(j)$ and $\hat{\rho}(j), j = 0, 1, 2, \ldots$, are the sample autocovariances and autocorrelations of the series $\{X_t\}$.

The program computes the coefficients ϕ_j for each set of lags such that

$$1 < l_1 < l_2 < l_3 \leq m$$

```
        < Finding best memory shortening polynomial>
BEST LONG-MEMORY LAG
   12
LAGGED AR COEFFICIENT
   9.778940E-01
RESIDUAL S.S./TOTAL S.S.
   3.668375E-03

BEST LONG-MEMORY LAG
   1
LAGGED AR COEFFICIENT
   7.024037E-01
RESIDUAL S.S./TOTAL S.S.
   4.838039E-01

    < Memory shortening is now complete>

COEFFICIENT OF B**j IN MEMORY-SHORTENING POLYNOMIAL,  j=0,1,... :
   1.0000    .0000    .0000    .0000    .0000
    .0000    .0000    .0000    .0000    .0000
    .0000    .0000   -.9779

   <Press any key to continue>
```

FIGURE 8.2. *Memory-shortening filter selected for DEATHS.DAT*

where m can be chosen to be either 13 or 26. It then selects the model for which the Yule-Walker estimate σ^2 is minimum and prints out the lags, coefficients and white noise variance for the fitted model.

A slower procedure chooses the lags and coefficients (computed from the Yule-Walker equations as above) which maximize the Gaussian likelihood of the observations. For this option the maximum lag m is 13.

The options are displayed in the Subset AR Menu (Figure 8.3) which appears on the screen when memory-shortening has been completed (or when you opt to by-pass memory shortening and fit a subset AR to the original (mean-corrected) data).

8.2   Running the Program

To determine an ARAR model for the given data set $\{Y_t\}$ and to use it to forecast future values of the series, we first read in the data set. Following the appearance on the screen of the Main Menu, we type **D** ↩ to select the option [**Determine the memory-shortening polynomial ...**] which then finds the best memory-shortening filter. After a short time delay the coefficients $1, \psi_1, \ldots, \psi_k$ of the chosen filter will be displayed on the screen. The memory shortened series is

$$S_t = Y_t + \psi_1 Y_{t-1} + \cdots + \psi_k Y_{t-k}.$$

```
MEAN OF SHORT-MEMORY SERIES   =     23.2217
LENGTH OF SHORT-MEMORY SERIES =     60
  SUBSET AR MENU :

  ┌─────────────────────────────────────────────┐
  │ Find the 4-coefficient Yule-Walker model with│
  │    minimum WN variance estimate (max lag = 13).│
  │ Find the 4-coefficient Yule-Walker model with │
  │    minimum WN variance estimate (max lag = 26).│
  │ Find the 4-coefficient Yule-Walker model with │
  │    maximum Gaussian likelihood (max lag = 13). │
  │ Return to main menu.                           │
  └─────────────────────────────────────────────┘

Optimal lags   :           1         3        12        13
Optimal coeffs :        .5915     .2093    -.3022     .2970
WN Variance    :    .12314E+06
COEFFICIENTS OF OVERALL WHITENING FILTER :
  1.0000      -.5915     .0000    -.2093     .0000
   .0000       .0000     .0000     .0000     .0000
   .0000       .0000    -.6757     .2814     .0000
   .2047       .0000     .0000     .0000     .0000
   .0000       .0000     .0000     .0000    -.2955
   .2904
```

FIGURE 8.3. *The four-coefficient autoregression fitted to the memory-shortened DEATHS.DAT series*

Type $\hookleftarrow$ and the Subset AR Menu will appear. The first option (selected by typing **F**) fits an autoregression with four non-zero coefficients to the mean-corrected series $X_t = S_t - \overline{S}$, choosing the lags and coefficients which minimize the Yule-Walker estimate of white noise variance. Type **F** and the optimal lags and corresponding coefficients in the model

$$X_t = \phi_1 X_{t-1} + \phi_{l_1} X_{t-l_1} + \phi_{l_2} X_{t-l_2} + \phi_{l_3} X_{t-l_3} + Z_t,$$

will be printed on the screen. The coefficients ξ_j of B^j in the overall whitening filter (B is the backward shift operator),

$$\xi(B) = (1 + \psi_1 B + \cdots + \psi_k B^k)(1 - \phi_1 B - \phi_{l_1} B^{l_1} - \phi_{l_2} B^{l_2} - \phi_{l_3} B^{l_3}),$$

are also printed.

Type $\hookleftarrow$ again and you will be asked for the number of future values of $\{Y_t\}$ to be predicted. Enter the required number and type $\hookleftarrow$ $\hookleftarrow$ to see the graph of the original data. Type $\hookleftarrow$ again and the predicted values will be added to the graph. Type $\hookleftarrow$ **C N** and you will be asked if you wish to file the predictors. Following this you will be returned to the Subset AR Menu, from which you may either select one of the other fitting options or return to the Main Menu from which you may leave the program.

EXAMPLE: To use the program *ARAR* to predict 24 values of the data file DEATHS.DAT, proceed as follows (starting from

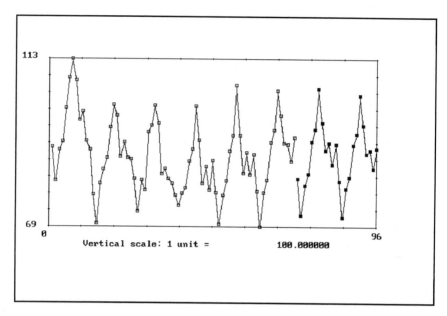

FIGURE 8.4. *The data set DEATHS.DAT with 24 predicted values*

the Main Menu, immediately after having read in the data file DEATHS.DAT).

Type **D** and the coefficients of the selected memory-shortening filter will appear. Figure 8.2 shows that the chosen filter is $(1 - .9779B^{12})$.

To continue, type ↵ **F**. The program then fits a four-coefficient AR model to the mean-corrected memory-shortened data, with maximum lag 13, selecting the model with minimum estimated white-noise variance. The fitted model is displayed in Figure 8.3.

To predict 24 future values of the series, type ↵ **24**↵ At this stage the screen will show the square root of the *observed* mean squared error of the one-step predictors of the data itself. To plot the predictors of future values type ↵ ↵ and you will see the original data with the 24 predictors plotted on the same graph as in Figure 8.4.

To exit from the program type ↵ **C N R x**.

9

LONGMEM

9.1 Introduction (*BD Section 13.2*)

The program *LONGMEM* is designed for simulation, model-fitting and prediction with ARIMA(p, d, q) processes, where $-.5 < d < .5$. Such processes, known as fractionally integrated ARMA processes, are stationary solutions of difference equations of the form

$$(1 - B)^d \phi(B) X_t = \theta(B) Z_t,$$

where $\phi(z)$ and $\theta(z)$ are polynomials of degrees p and q respectively, satisfying

$$\phi(z) \neq 0 \quad \text{and} \quad \theta(z) \neq 0 \quad \text{for all } |z| \text{ such that } |z| \leq 1,$$

B is the backward shift operator ($B^k X_t = X_{t-k}$ and $B^k Z_t = Z_{t-k}$) and $\{Z_t\}$ is a white noise sequence with mean 0 and variance σ^2. The operator $(1 - B)^d$ is defined by the binomial expansion,

$$(1 - B)^d = \sum_{j=0}^{\infty} \pi_j B^j,$$

where

$$\pi_j = \prod_{0 < k \leq j} \frac{k - 1 - d}{k}, \quad j = 0, 1, \ldots.$$

The autocorrelation $\rho(h)$ at lag h of an ARIMA(p, d, q) process with $-.5 < d < .5$ is asymptotically (as $h \to \infty$) of the form $(Const)h^{2d-1}$. This converges to zero as $h \to \infty$ at a much slower rate than $\rho(h)$ for an ARMA process which is bounded in absolute value by $(Const)r^h$, with $r < 1$. Consequently fractionally integrated ARMA processes are said to have "long memory". In contrast, stationary processes whose ACF converges to 0 rapidly, such as ARMA processes, are said to have "short memory".

To begin a session with the program *LONGMEM*, double click on the icon labelled *longmem* in the *itsm* window (or in DOS type LONGMEM↩ from the C:\ITSMW directory). You will see a title screen followed by a brief explanation of *LONGMEM*, and will then be given the choice of entering both data and a model or just a model. If the option [Input data and model] is selected, you will be asked to choose the data file and whether or not you wish to subtract the sample mean from the data. Type S unless you wish to assume that the data is generated by a zero-mean model. You must then

choose to [**Enter** model from keyboard] or [**R**ead model from a file]. Choose
the latter if the required model has been entered previously and saved in a
file. To enter a model from the keyboard, type **E** and follow the program
prompts. These will ask for the parameter d (between $-.5$ and $.5$), the
order of the autoregression p, the AR coefficients, $\phi_1, \ldots, \phi_p$, the order of
the moving average q, the MA coefficients, $\theta_1, \ldots, \theta_q$ and finally the white
noise variance σ^2. The following message will then be displayed on your
screen:

```
The model autocovariance function is calculated from

GAMMA(h)= SUM [psi(j)*psi(k)*gamma(h+j-k)]

where gamma is the ACVF of fractionally integrated
WN with index d, and j and k run from  0 to N.  The
default value of N is 50.  You may wish to increase
N if you have an autoregressive zero very close to
the unit circle.
```

The exact autocovariance function of the model can be expressed as

$$\gamma_X(h) = \sum_{j=0}^{\infty} \sum_{k=0}^{\infty} \psi_j \psi_k \gamma_Y(h+j-k),$$

where $\sum_{i=0}^{\infty} \psi_i z^i = \theta(z)/\phi(z)$, $|z| \leq 1$, and $\gamma_Y(\cdot)$ is the autocovariance
function of fractionally integrated white noise with parameters d and σ^2
(see *BD* , equations (13.2.8) and (13.2.9)). As the screen message indicates,
the upper limits of summation are replaced in the program by N, where N
has the default value of 50. If $\phi(z)$ has a zero close to the unit circle you may
wish to increase the value of N (up to 200) to reduce the truncation error.
After entering **N** press $\hookleftarrow$ to view a summary of the current model stored
in the program and then press $\hookleftarrow$ to see the Estimation and Prediction
Menu (Figure 9.1).

9.2   Parameter Estimation (*BD p.527–532*)

LONGMEM estimates the parameters, $\beta = (d, \phi_1, \ldots, \phi_p, \theta_1, \ldots, \theta_q)'$ and
σ^2 of a fractionally integrated model by maximizing the Whittle approximation, L_W, to the likelihood function. This is equivalent to minimization
of

$$-2\ln(L_W) = n\ln(2\pi) + 2n\ln\sigma + \sigma^{-2} \sum_j \frac{I_n(\omega_j)}{g(\omega_j; \beta)} + \sum_j \ln g(\omega_,; \beta),$$

where I_n is the periodogram, $\sigma^2 g$ is the model spectral density and $\sum_j$ denotes the sum over all non-zero Fourier frequencies, $\omega_j = 2\pi j/n \in (-\pi, \pi]$.

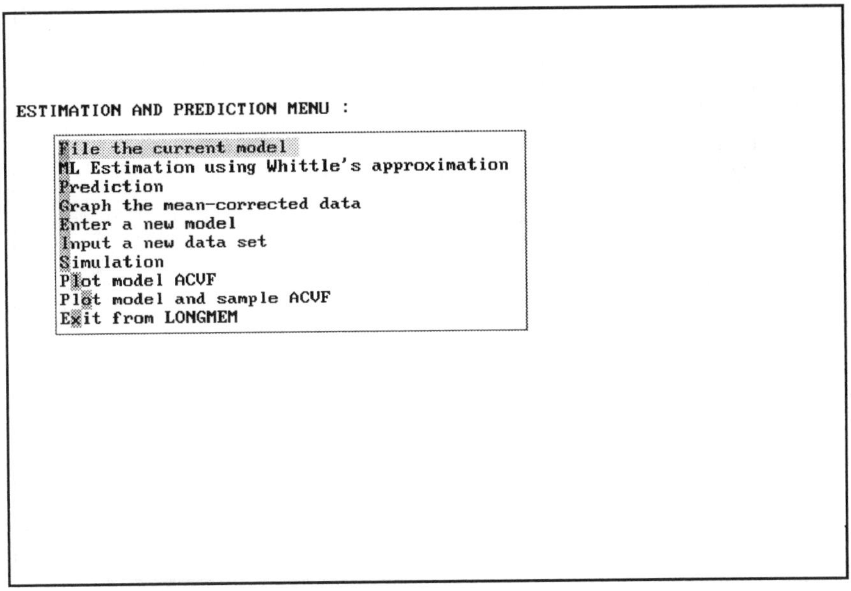

ESTIMATION AND PREDICTION MENU :

```
File the current model
ML Estimation using Whittle's approximation
Prediction
Graph the mean-corrected data
Enter a new model
Input a new data set
Simulation
Plot model ACVF
Plot model and sample ACVF
Exit from LONGMEM
```

FIGURE 9.1. *The Estimation and Prediction Menu of* LONGMEM

The option [ML Estimation using Whittle's approximation] performs the necessary optimization.

EXAMPLE: Start the program *LONGMEM* and press ↩ ↩ to clear the first two displays. Type **I** to input both data and a model. After selecting the data set E1321.DAT, subtract its mean by typing **S**. Enter the ARIMA$(0, .3, 1)$ model with $\theta_1 = .2$ and $\sigma^2 = 1.0$ by typing **E** .3↩ 0↩ 1↩ .2↩ 1.0↩ . Then type **N** to use the default value of $N = 50$. At this point the model and the corresponding value of $-2\ln(L_W)$ (where L_W is the Whittle likelihood) will be displayed. Press ↩ to view the Estimation and Prediction Menu and type **M** to estimate the parameters of the model. You must then choose whether to optimize with respect to all parameters or to keep d fixed. The usual choice (unless d is known or has been otherwise estimated) is [Optimize with respect to all parameters]. After typing **O**, specify the optimization step size as 0.1 by typing .1↩ . Once the optimization with this (rather large) step size is complete, optimization should be repeated with step sizes .01 and then .001. This leads to the model displayed in Figure 9.2.

```
CURRENT MODEL PARAMETERS ARE:
 MA COEFFICIENTS
     .8115001
 ORDER OF DIFFERENCING
     .3950000
 WN VARIANCE
 .5144705E+00
-2ln(L) (Whittle)      =     .429278E+03
AKAIKE AIC STATISTIC   =     .435278E+03

   <Press any key to continue>
```

FIGURE 9.2. *The model fitted by maximum likelihood*

9.3   Prediction $\left(\textit{BD p.533–534}\right)$

Select the option [**Prediction**] to forecast future values of the time series using the fitted model. Assuming that the observations $X_1, \ldots, X_n$ ($X_1 - m, \ldots, X_n - m$ if you chose to subtract the sample mean m) were generated by the fitted model, *LONGMEM* predicts X_{n+h} as the linear combination $P_n(X_{n+h})$ of $1, X_1, \ldots, X_n$ which minimizes the mean squared error $E(X_{n+h} - P_n(X_{n+h}))^2$. The Durbin-Levinson algorithm (*BD Section 5.2*) is used to compute the predictors from the data and the model autocovariance function.

> EXAMPLE: Starting from the Estimation and Prediction Menu with the mean-corrected data set and model just fitted to it, type **P** 40↩ to predict the next 40 observations of E1321.DAT. The first 20 predicted values and the corresponding values of SQRT(MSE) will appear on the screen. Press ↩ to see the next 20. Type ↩ **Y** ↩ ↩ and you will see a graph of the original data with the forty predicted values appended (Figure 9.3). Notice that the predictors are converging to the sample mean $m = -.0434$ quite slowly. If however we fit an ARMA(3,3) model to the mean-corrected data, we find that the corresponding predictors converge to m much more rapidly.

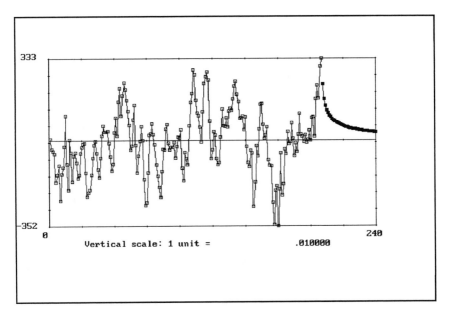

FIGURE 9.3. *Predictors of E1321.DAT and the values of SQRT(MSE)*

9.4   Simulation

The option [Simulation] of the Estimation and Prediction Menu of *LONG-MEM* can be used for generating realizations of a fractionally integrated ARMA process. To generate such a realization type **S** and then **Y** when asked if you wish to continue with the simulation. The program will ask you to enter the number of data points required (up to 1000 for *ITSM41* or 20000 for *ITSM50*) and a random number seed (an integer with fewer than 10 digits). The simulated data set will be stored in *LONGMEM* , overwriting any data previously stored in the program. You will not be given the option of subtracting the sample mean since the simulated series *is* generated by a model with zero mean.

> EXAMPLE: To generate 200 data points from the model fitted above to E1321.DAT, start in the Estimation and Prediction Menu and type **S Y** 200↩ 7486↩ . (You can get an independent realization by choosing some number other than 7486 as the random number seed.) Return to the Estimation and Prediction Menu and type **G** to graph the simulated data (Figure 9.4).

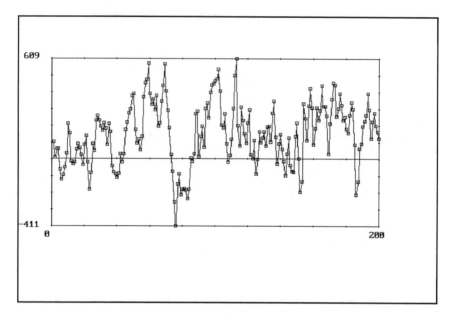

FIGURE 9.4. *Data generated from a fractionally integrated model*

9.5   Plotting the model and sample ACVF

The option [Plot model ACVF] of the Estimation and Prediction Menu allows you to plot the autocovariance function of the model. Provided data have also been read in (or simulated), the model ACVF can be overlayed with the sample ACVF using the option [Plot model and sample ACVF]. If the data have not been mean-corrected they are assumed to have come from a zero-mean series and the sample ACVF is computed as $\hat{\gamma}(h) = \sum_{t=1}^{n-h} X_{t+h}X_t/n, \ h \geq 0$.

> EXAMPLE: Continuing with the previous example, return to the Estimation and Prediction Menu and type **o**. The model ACVF should then appear on your screen. Press ↵ to superimpose the sample ACVF (Figure 9.5).

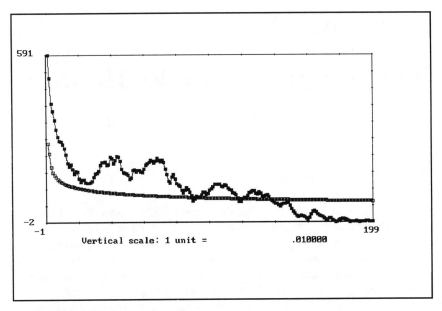

FIGURE 9.5. *The model ACVF and sample ACVF of the generated data*

Appendix A

The Screen Editor WORD6

By Anthony E. Brockwell

A.1 Basic Editing

The cursor can be moved with the four cursor control keys. The <End> key moves the cursor to the end of the line, and the <Home> key to the first character of the line. <PgUp> and <PgDn> move the cursor 22 lines up and 22 lines down, respectively. <Ctrl>-<Home> and <Ctrl>-<End> move the cursor to the beginning and end of the text respectively (<Ctrl>-<Home> means holding down the <Ctrl> key while pressing the <Home> key).

The backspace key <←> (upper right of keyboard) deletes the character at the cursor position and moves the cursor back one space. The <Del> key deletes the character at the cursor position without moving the cursor. To merge two lines, move the cursor to the far left of the screen (using <Home> and then the left arrow) and press the <←> key. The line will then be moved up and put on the end of the line above.

The <Ins> key toggles insert and overwrite modes. In insert mode characters will be inserted into the text at the current cursor position. In overwrite mode they replace the old character and the <Enter> key moves the cursor to the next line without inserting a new line. At the bottom of the screen, a message shows whether you are in insert or overwrite mode.

A.2 Alternate Keys

To perform special functions, *WORD6* makes use of the <Alt> key. The <Alt> key works in the same way as the <Shift> key. To enter <Alt>-X, for example, press the <Alt> key, and while still holding it down, press X. Note — either X or x will do, as the computer does not differentiate between upper and lower case alternate keys.

The two most essential <Alt>-keys are <Alt>-R and <Alt>-W. To read an ASCII file into the editor, type <Alt>-R, and then enter the name of the file to be read in. (Alternatively, you can type WORD6 FNAME to begin editing an existing file called FNAME.) When you have finished editing or creating a file, <Alt>-W can be used to write the file to disk.

To exit from *WORD6*, enter <Alt>-X. If you have edited a file without saving it, you will be asked whether you really want to exit without saving the file. To save the file, answer n and then use <Alt>-W.

<Alt>-D and <Alt>-I can be used to delete and insert large sections of text quickly. <Alt>-D deletes the entire line at the current cursor position and moves all the text below it up one line. <Alt>-I inserts a blank line above the current cursor position.

If you have a color monitor, <Alt>-Z can be used to change the screen color.

A.3   Printing a File

To print a file, use <Alt>-W as though writing a file. Then when prompted for the file name, enter LPT1 (or possibly LPT2 if you have two printers). This is a DOS filename which allows the printer to be treated as though it were a file.

To make use of special printer control codes (for underlining, bold-face, etc.) enter these codes directly into the document. Use <Alt>-0 to redefine <Alt>-(1-9) by ASCII code, and then any combination of control codes can be sent to the printer.

A.4   Merging Two or More Files

The <Alt>-R command does not replace the old document with a new one. It merges the new file into the current text. If there is no current text — as after using <Alt>-N or just after entering *WORD6* from the DOS prompt — the new file will obviously not be merged. For example, to merge a fifty line file between the tenth and eleventh lines of an old sixty line file, read in the sixty line file, insert a blank line between its tenth and eleventh lines, position the cursor anywhere on the blank line, and then read in the fifty line file using <Alt>-R. To merge the new file onto the end of the old one, just position the cursor at the end of the old one using <Ctrl>-<End>, press ↵ (optional), and read in the new one.

A.5   Margins and Left and Centre Justification

<Alt>-L and <Alt>-P set left and right margins, respectively. The margin will be set at wherever the cursor is when the key is pressed. The shading over the tab settings will change to show only what is included between the left and right margin. Text will automatically wrap around to the left margin on the next line if the cursor moves past the right margin on the current line. To left-justify text, press <Ctrl>-L (like <Alt>-L, except use

the <Ctrl> key instead of the <Alt> key). The current line will be moved so that it starts right on the left margin. <Ctrl>-M will centre-justify text by placing it centrally between the right and left margins.

A.6   Tab Settings

<Alt>-T sets or removes a tab setting. If there is a tab setting at the current cursor position, it will be removed, if there is no tab setting, one will be added. Tab settings are indicated by little white hats at the bottom of the screen. When the tab key is pressed, the cursor will automatically move to the next tab position.

> EXAMPLE: To get rid of the next tab setting, press the tab key to move there, and then press <Alt>-T to remove the setting. The hat marking that tab setting will disappear.

A.7   Block Commands

Large sections of text can be moved or erased as follows using the <Alt>-M command. Move to the first line of the section to be marked and press <Alt>-M. Then move to the last line and press <Alt>-M again. The entire block between and including the two lines will change color to show that it has been marked. After marking a block, the <Alt>-E and <Alt>-C commands can be used. <Alt>-E deletes the entire block. <Alt>-C makes a second copy of the block after the line at the current cursor position. For instance, to delete the entire text, press <Ctrl>-<Home>, <Alt>-M, <Ctrl>-<End>, <Alt>-M and then <Alt>-E will erase the entire text.

Note:

1. Only one block can exist at once. <Alt>-C makes a copy of the old block and leaves it marked.

2. To unmark a block, press <Alt>-M. If a block already exists, <Alt>-M removes the marking.

3. To move a section of text, mark it, move the cursor to the line before the new desired position and press <Alt>-C, and then press <Alt>-E to get rid of the old block.

If you wish to write only part of the text to a file, mark the required block, and then press <Alt>-B. You will be prompted for the file name.

Vertical blocks may also be manipulated by using <Alt>-F. Mark each end of the block by pressing <Alt>-F. To delete a marked block press <Alt>-G. To move a marked block to the right or left, press <Alt>-U and use the arrow keys. When the marked block is appropriately located press ↩ . To unmark the block press <Alt>-F again.

A.8   Searching

To locate a certain word or set of characters in a file, use <Alt>-R to read the file into *WORD6*. Then type <Alt>-S. You will be prompted for a string to search for and what to replace it with. If you want to search and not replace, just press ↪ when asked **Replace with** ?. You will then be asked the question **Ignore case (Y/N)** ?. (If you answer **N** then a search for *The* will not find *the*.) The cursor will then be moved to the first occurrence of the string after the current cursor position. If the string is not found in the text, the cursor will reappear at the end of the file. Searching and replacing is always global, but can be aborted with the <Esc> key. Each time the string is found, you will be prompted as to whether or not to replace it. If you enter **N** or **n**, the search will go on to the next occurrence of the string. Since a search always starts at the current cursor position, it is usually a good idea to go to the beginning of the text using <Ctrl>-<Home> before carrying out a search.

> EXAMPLE: To replace every occurrence of *this* in the text with *that*, go to the beginning of the text by pressing <Ctrl>-<Home>. Then press <Alt>-S. Then enter **this** and then enter **that**. *WORD6* will then give the prompt **Replace (Y/N)?** for every occurrence of this in the text. If you enter **y** or **Y** the *this* at the cursor position will be changed to a *that*.
>
> <Alt>-Q repeats the last search, and does not replace.

Instead of searching only within a file, you can search through specified files in a directory with the <Alt>-J command.

> EXAMPLE: To replace every occurrence of *xaxis* by *yaxis* in the files with names ending in *.for* in the current directory, type **word6** from the DOS prompt and then type <Alt>-J. When **File specification** is requested, type *.for. Then proceed as in the previous example, typing **xaxis** (the string to be replaced) and **yaxis** (the replacement string) as required. Each time the search reaches the end of a file you will be given the opportunity to save the new file with the specified changes.

A.9   Special Characters

By making use of <Alt>-(1-9), *WORD6* can access characters which cannot normally be accessed from the keyboard. Each time *WORD6* is run, a set of some of the more useful Greek letters are loaded into the keys <Alt>-1, <Alt>-2, ... <Alt>-9. However these can be redefined by ASCII code by pressing <Alt>-0.

A box can be created by using ASCII codes 192, 196, 217, 179, 218 and 191. These each display a different segment of the box. Press <Alt>-0 and enter these six numbers for six of the nine <Alt>-keys. Then by pressing <Alt>-(1-9), these segments of the box can be put on the screen and edited to the correct position.

A.10 Function Keys

Function can be defined to be any string of up to forty characters. It can save time to redefine commonly used phrases as function keys (for instance write(*,*) in Fortran.) Press <F10> to redefine a function key. When asked which one to define, press the function key you wish to assign a string to.[1] Then enter the string. You may define up to nine different function keys at once.

A.11 Editing Information

At the bottom of the screen is a list of parameters. At the far left is a message F1 = Help. Next to that is either Insert or Overwrite. This is the current editing mode, which can be toggled using the <Ins> key. Next to that a number displays the column number of the cursor (anywhere from 1 to 65535). At the far right are two numbers, separated by a slash. The number on the left of the slash is the number of the line at which the cursor is currently located. The number on the right of the slash is the total number of lines in the document.

On the line above all this information, a series of hats may be displayed. These are all the tab settings. In addition to the tab settings, this line is shaded to show the left and right margins.

---

[1]The tab key will appear as a small circle when used in the definition of a function key, and will be decoded when the function key is pressed while editing. Thus function key definitions including tabs will be placed on the screen as though the tab key is pressed at the position it appears on the screen. It is not converted into a set number of spaces to be put on the screen.

Appendix B

Data Sets

USPOP.DAT Population of United States at ten-year intervals, 1790–1980 (U.S.Bureau of the Census). *BD Example 1.1.2.*

STRIKES.DAT Strikes in the U.S.A., 1951–1980 (Bureau of Labor Statistics). *BD Example 1.1.3.*

SUNSPOTS.DAT The Wolfer sunspot numbers, 1770–1869. *BD Example 1.1.5.*

DEATHS.DAT Monthly accidental deaths in the U.S.A., 1973–1978 (National Safety Council). *BD Example 1.1.6.*

AIRPASS.DAT International airline passenger monthly totals (in thousands), Jan. 49 – Dec. 60. From Box and Jenkins (*Time Series Analysis: Forecasting and Control, 1970*). *BD Example 9.2.2.*

E911.DAT 200 simulated values of an ARIMA(1,1,0) process. *BD Example 9.1.1.*

E921.DAT 200 simulated values of an AR(2) process. *BD Example 9.2.1.*

E923.DAT 200 simulated values of an ARMA(2,1) process. *BD Example 9.2.3.*

E951.DAT 200 simulated values of an ARIMA(1,2,1) process. *BD Example 9.5.1.*

E1021.DAT Sinusoid plus simulated Gaussian white noise. *BD Example 10.2.1.*

E1042.DAT 160 simulated values of an MA(1) process. *BD Example 10.4.2.*

E1062.DAT 400 simulated values of an MA(1) process. *BD Example 10.6.2.*

LEAD.DAT Leading Indicator Series from Box and Jenkins (*Time Series Analysis: Forecasting and Control, 1970*). *BD Example 11.2.2.*

SALES.DAT Sales Data from Box and Jenkins (*Time Series Analysis: Forecasting and Control, 1970*). *BD Example 11.2.2.*

E1321.DAT 200 values of a simulated fractionally differenced MA(1) series. *BD Example 13.2.1.*

E1331.DAT 200 values of a simulated MA(1) series with standard Cauchy white noise. *BD Example 13.3.2.*

E1332.DAT 200 values of a simulated AR(1) series with standard Cauchy white noise. *BD Example 13.3.2.*

APPA.DAT Lake level of Lake Huron in feet (reduced by 570), 1875–1972. *BD Appendix Series A.*

APPB.DAT Dow Jones Utilities Index, Aug.28–Dec.18, 1972. *BD Appendix Series B.*

APPC.DAT Private Housing Units Started, U.S.A. (monthly). From the Makridakis competition, series 922. *BD Appendix Series C.*

APPD.DAT Industrial Production, Austria (quarterly). From the Makridakis competition, Series 337. *BD Appendix Series D.*

APPE.DAT Industrial Production, Spain (monthly). From the Makridakis competition, Series 868. *BD Appendix Series E.*

APPF.DAT General Index of Industrial Production (monthly). From the Makridakis competition, Series 904. *BD Appendix, Series F.*

APPG.DAT Annual Canadian Lynx Trappings, 1821–1934. *BD Appendix Series G.*

APPH.DAT Annual Mink Trappings, 1848–1911. *BD Appendix Series H.*

APPI.DAT Annual Muskrat Trappings, 1848–1911. *BD Appendix Series I.*

APPJ.DAT Simulated input series for transfer function model. *BD Appendix Series J.*

APPK.DAT Simulated output series for transfer function model. *BD Appendix Series K.*

LRES.DAT Whitened Leading Indicator Series obtained by fitting an MA(1) to the mean-corrected differenced series LEAD.DAT. *BD Section 13.1.*

SRES.DAT Residuals obtained from the mean-corrected and differenced SALES.DAT data when the filter used for whitening the mean-corrected differenced LEAD.DAT series is applied. *BD Section 3.1.*

APPJK2.DAT The two series APPJ and APPK (see above) in bivariate format for analysis by ARVEC and BURG.

LS2.DAT Lead-Sales data in bivariate format for analysis by ARVEC and BURG.

GNFP.DAT Australian gross non-farm product at average 1984/5 prices in millions of dollars. September quarter, 1959, through March quarter, 1990 (Australian Bureau of Statistics).

FINSERV.DAT Australian expenditure on financial services in millions of dollars. September quarter, 1969, through March quarter, 1990 (Australian Bureau of Statistics).

BEER.DAT Australian monthly beer production in megalitres, including ale and stout and excluding beverages with alcohol percentage less than 1.15. January, 1956, through April, 1990 (Australian Bureau of Statistics).

ELEC.DAT Australian monthly electricity production in millions of kilowatt hours. January, 1956, through April, 1990 (Australian Bureau of Statistics).

CHOCS.DAT Australian monthly chocolate-based confectionery production in tonnes. July, 1957, through October, 1990 (Australian Bureau of Statistics).

IMPORTS.DAT Australian imports of all goods and services in millions of Australian dollars at average 1984/85 prices. September quarter, 1959, through December quarter, 1990 (Australian Bureau of Statistics).

Index